PUBLIC SPEAKING

The Best Solutions to Perform the Speech of Your Life

(Find Your Style and Improve Your Communication and Social Skills)

Richard Martin

Published by Andrew Zen

Richard Martin

All Rights Reserved

Public Speaking: The Best Solutions to Perform the Speech of Your Life (Find Your Style and Improve Your Communication and Social Skills)

ISBN 978-1-77485-231-6

All rights reserved. No part of this guide may be reproduced in any form without permission in writing from the publisher except in the case of brief quotations embodied in critical articles or reviews.

Legal & Disclaimer

The information contained in this book is not designed to replace or take the place of any form of medicine or professional medical advice. The information in this book has been provided for educational and entertainment purposes only.

The information contained in this book has been compiled from sources deemed reliable, and it is accurate to the best of the Author's knowledge; however, the Author cannot guarantee its accuracy and validity and cannot be held liable for any errors or omissions. Changes are periodically made to this book. You must consult your doctor or get professional medical advice before using any of the suggested remedies, techniques, or information in this book.

Upon using the information contained in this book, you agree to hold harmless the Author from and against any damages, costs, and expenses, including any legal fees potentially resulting from the application of any of the information provided by this guide. This disclaimer applies to any damages or injury caused by the use and application, whether directly or indirectly, of any advice or information presented, whether for breach of contract, tort, negligence, personal injury, criminal intent, or under any other cause of action.

You agree to accept all risks of using the information presented inside this book. You need to consult a professional medical practitioner in order to ensure you are both able and healthy enough to participate in this program.

TABLE OF CONTENTS

INTRODUCTION 1

CHAPTER 1: MY (BAD!) EXPERIENCE WITH PUBLIC SPEAKING 2

CHAPTER 2: WHY GIVING A GREAT PRESENTATION IS SO IMPORTANT 8

CHAPTER 3: PUBLIC SPEAKING ANXIETY, FEAR AND CAUSES 14

CHAPTER 4: THE PHYSIOLOGY AND PUBLIC SPEAKING 19

CHAPTER 5: ANALYZING YOUR AUDIENCE 29

CHAPTER 6: THE STRUCTURE AND OUTLINE FOR A GREAT SPEECH 36

CHAPTER 7: GENERATING INTEREST 39

CHAPTER 8: WHY PUBLIC SPEAKING? 46

CHAPTER 9: THE NATURE OF THE BEAST: PUBLIC SPEAKING AND STAGE FRIGHT 64

CHAPTER 10: WEAR YOUR HEART ON THE SLEEVES 69

CHAPTER 11: THE FIRST HONEY 72

CHAPTER 12: OVERCOMING OBSTACLES 79

CHAPTER 13: HOW TO DELIVER A SPEECH 87

CHAPTER 14: BUILD CONFIDENCE 94

CHAPTER 15: PUBLIC SPEAKING IS EASY... IT IS ALL IN YOUR MIND! 103

CHAPTER 16: PRELIMINARY NOTES FOR YOUR SPEECH . 109

CHAPTER 17: NOBODY IS PERFECT - MISTAKES ARE GUARANTEED.. 112

CHAPTER 18: HOW TO GIVE A DYNAMIC SPEECH 127

CHAPTER 19: THE FIRST STEP IS STARTING 131

CHAPTER 20: EVELIUATION 136

CHAPTER 21: PROFESSIONAL SPEAKERS' REAL MESSAGE 147

CHAPTER 22: HUMOR... 163

CHAPTER 23: THE SPEECH OPENING: A SPARK IS THE BEST START.. 175

CONCLUSION... 184

Introduction

Do you ever think that someone speaks in front of a lot of people and seem so confident? Or is he afraid of everyone else? That's what you probably think when you first hear someone express their thoughts clearly and are able communicate his message effectively to others.

However, if anxiety or fear of speaking up is a concern, it's possible to think that you won't be like them and that you will remain inside your shell.

Chapter 1: My (Bad!) Experience With Public Speaking

I vividly remember being a junior at an upscale high school in Texas and having to present in front my science class. The teacher asked students to make an invention and illustrate it on paper. They then had to color it and present it in front of the class. I thought deeply about myself and decided to create something I could be proud of, not something I wanted. That was my main concern. I didn't want students to get mad at me, or be laughed at. I think all that thinking only made the experience worse. It turned out to have been one of the worst days of mine.

I sat in class this day and was rolling the pencil between each of my two hands. My hands started to sweat, and I could see the clock ticking continually. Each tick meant that I was getting less time to finish my assignment. My mind became blurred and my body felt even worse. I began to feel a sudden pain in my chest, lasting only a couple of seconds. This pain is indicative of severe anxiety. I started to take deeper breaths, in an attempt to calm down. I was too fixated on how to present myself and survive scrutiny by around thirty students that I lost my sense of time.

My stomach ached when I heard my teacher stand up, pull up his sleeves, yell, "Five Minutes left, class!" I was sucked in. I had not started the assignment. Although I was intelligent, my fear about public speaking crippled the rest of my intellect.

In an attempt to avoid being the only student not to complete the assignment and possibly shamed in front the class, I designed a robot. Though a robot may not seem like a very impressive invention, mine was. My robot could make sandwiches, and it could churn them through its abdomen. I raced to complete my assignment before the next student presented. I rushed, even more so because I could be the first student to present.

Fortunately, I wasn't selected to be one of the first sheep given to the wolves. (This analogy illustrates how much I hate public speaking). A classmate who was short, fragile, and young was chosen. Although she presented with great eloquence, her invention was described persuasively. The object she created was a pink, circular camera. She explained that the camera wasn't special. She said that this camera "has the ability of enlarging an image one thousand-fold." It comes equipped with both normal and microscopical lenses. The microscopic lens lets us zoom in on objects we can't see with our naked eye, and then take photos to transfer them back to our personal computers." This was how she made something ordinary extraordinary. The power and versatility of speech, I thought.

I was amazed at her creativity and the coolness of having such a great camera. I also began to consider how high she had set their bar. Sometimes we do things we perceive as horrible in ourselves; other times we do things we perceive as awful compared to others. I thought my presentation would be an example. There was this bright girl with some confidence, presenting an object I found very fascinating. And there I was, waiting, sweaty hands in my palms, to present my sandwich making robot.

I knew I was going to be up soon because the teacher called me randomly. While I waited for the teacher to call me, I spoke with myself to calm my nerves. I said, "You'll do fine. Many students are taking this class, however most of them don't pay attention. You'll be fine. You should only be up there for five minutes. Concentrate and complete the tasks. Once you do, your life will resume as normal as it was prior to this class.

However, it didn't seem to work for long. My heart began to beat faster, my hands began trembled, and my ears started to feel hot when I was called by my teacher. I stood up slowly, and began to walk towards the front of the class.

I remained composed while introducing my self, and managed to get through my name (and classification) with ease. I looked at the paper in front of my face and said, "Here is our class!" I turned my paper over and showed it to them. I found a typical robot design on the paper. As every other robot that we know, its arms, legs, feets, head and abdomen were drawn in boxes. The robot's stomach was represented by a circular symbolizing a hole. You can guess what that circle represented. It was the place where the robot funneled its sandwiches to its owner, or to whomever the owner wanted to feed. I felt very uncomfortable as the students started to laugh at me. Then, I heard my teacher exclaim: "Jesus Christ!" Students exploded in laughter. My face started feeling swollen. It was stingingly achy. At that point, I knew my face was about to become red. I tried my best to keep cool but failed. I was ashamed of my actions.

My face turned completely ruddy and I began to sweat profusely, right under my hairline. It was worse, my mouth dried so much that I couldn't speak properly. My heart was beating fast and hard.

All eyes were on you. How ironic! Students were looking at their phones during presentations that were worthy of their attention. My presentation was clearly not a good one. All students were focused on me. It was all too much. I gave up at about the 2:25 mark. He slightly nodded his head as if to understand that I was feeling the pressure to leave the class because of the recent breakdown. I left class and didn't come back to class until the next morning.

This is a widespread fear among students. But, it's not something that can be avoided. In order to succeed, you must be able and willing to share your knowledge with others. We can't hide from fear or run away. We have to face it. It will take time to overcome your fears. It's possible.

Chapter 2: Why giving a great presentation is so important

You are probably well aware of how important it is to give a great talk. To help motivate you and share all the advantages of being a great presenter, I listed these reasons:

This skill set is highly in demand and well-paying. A public speaker who is a master at giving speeches can earn six-figures. This book will not guarantee you a place in the top-tier of public speakers. But if you become better at giving presentations, it will allow you to eventually join this high-value segment. While six figures per talk may seem like a faraway dream, it is not unreasonable to consider that your career can be improved by being a great presenter. The advice contained in this book will help you to achieve promotions, better jobs, and other opportunities.

The ability to be a skilled presenter can be applied to many other areas. One example of this is sales. Being able to give presentations well is very similar in many ways to how you would approach sales situations such a cold call, business pitches, one on one selling, etc. You must present your ideas and yourself. You will be able to use the skills developed in this book to excel in other roles, which can also be high-value and money-making. You will see improvements in your ability to communicate with customers, sales, management, marketing and customer service. Do you like the idea of hitting two birds with a single stone? Aiming for half a dozen makes it even more enjoyable.

Making presentations can be used as a tool to help achieve other goals. Imagine being in a workplace where someone has to pitch a presentation about the new product your company is working on. You may be willing to give a presentation if you believe the product has future value. This is not because you are passionate about the product, but rather because it can help you become familiar with it. A presentation is an excellent way to learn, revise and remember a topic.

Relax. Relax. Take your stress off.

No doubt, you fear the worst. That is why you are reading this book.

Imagine the scene. You are at crunch-time and your peers are looking at. It isn't working as well or as efficiently as you want it to. And you are worried about the presentation. Now you feel some nerves starting to show up, which can turn into a knot in your stomach that spreads throughout your body. You don't know what to do next and your brain is unable to concentrate. Your forehead becomes swollen and you feel desperate for a sudden emergency to end this torture.

I'm not lying, it happens. This does not have to happen to anyone.

However, the above scenario holds a key lesson.

Don't allow emotions and stress to overwhelm you.

Below are three reasons why emotional stress management and awareness are essential to delivering a great presentation.

Stress and/or negative emotional overwhelm can quickly spiral. Although it may seem small, stress and/or any negative emotional overwhelm can quickly become a major problem.

A calm, relaxed state of mind leads to a calm and relaxed delivery. This will allow your audience to better understand you, which will result in them being more likely to listen to you and take the actions that you want.

People won't take you or your presentation as seriously if it looks nervous.

So how can we manage to relax, no matter how important or inexperienced, and keep our minds free from the pressures of life?

Breathe. This is a crucial step. Be sure to take deep, controlled breathes before you begin your presentation. Doing this for only a few seconds will help your mind and spirit "settle."

Take a few moments to pause throughout your presentation. This will help you "land" your ideas with your audience. Additionally, it gives you the chance to breathe again. Also, if you feel overwhelmed at any time, use this sign to stop and breathe.

If you have had experience with meditation, or have more time, you might be able to meditate briefly before your presentation. You can make a difference by sitting down for 10 mins in a comfortable posture and focusing on the breath.

Take care of your lifestyle, especially close to the time of presentation. Well-being, good sleep, exercising, and eating a healthy meal all contribute to your emotional stability as well as your ability to manage and control stress.

Even though it's helpful to be mindful of your breathing and relax, don't let that stop you from presenting with a focused, upbeat energy.

Chapter 3: Public Speaking Anxiety, Fear and Causes

It is important to understand what caused your fear or anxiety when you speak in public. Was there a traumatic experience at school? Maybe your self-confidence was affected at work and at home. No matter the reason, you must find out what it is and then use the knowledge to overcome your fear of speaking before a crowd. Below is a list with common anxiety and fears about public speaking.

Repeatedly traumatizing experiences in speaking and selfexpression

Sometimes traumatizing incidents in childhood cause people to repress their ability of speaking and hearing. These incidents are often accepted as normal or overlooked in a child's daily life. These traumas can be repeated and cause the child to lose their self-confidence. This is what they remember growing up.

Consider the following example.

Bobby is not a very good speaker, but his goal is to be one. Bobby was six when he entered his school's speech competition. Bobby trained hard every night to win that competition. Gary, the school bully, also signed up. Gary teased Bobby and made fun of him, telling him each day that Bobby was going forget his speech. Gary made Bobby feel bullied and discouraged daily. Gary made fun at Bobby every day, but it wasn't caught on the teachers' radars. If they did, they weren't able to do enough to correct the damage Gary was slowly causing to Bobby.

Bobby was nervous the day before the contest. Bobby was nervous and tried to remember the advice of his parents about staying calm. But all he could recall was how Gary had teased, mocked, and tainted. Bobby was sweating excessively when he was ready to step up onto the stage. He was able deliver the first part without making any mistakes. But, in the middle, he thought back to the bullying that Gary had done for him the previous few days. He lost track of all the things he had done and began stuttering. At first, there was only a faint squeak of laughter. The teachers tried to quieten the students, but they failed miserably. Poor Bobby was stuttering, and had difficulty finishing his speech. The school assembly roared in laughter.

You can see how Gary made an impact on Bobbys speech by repeating his actions. Bobby would probably have managed his speech if Gary had not continued to tease and taunt him. Bobby learned that speaking was not something he could do because of repeated traumatizing experiences. Bobby's humiliation at Gary's taunts was what triggered his fear. He didn't fear public speaking but the fear that he would fail and make a fool of him.

If you have had any similar experiences as Bobby, it is likely that these experiences were what caused your anxiety and fear of public speaking.

Minimal to no socialization

People who don't have enough socialization opportunities and the time they do, tend to grow up as shy children. They have little experience with socializing with peers and other people so they can be naturally anxious when they have to speak in public.

If you don't have many friends, or if your contacts with your peers and neighbor are very limited, this could be the reason for your public-speaking anxiety. It is difficult to be heard in public. Your body responds by producing adrenaline and sweat.

Pessimism

Public speaking fears are not only caused by external or environmental factors. But internal factors like self-talk, pessimism, and constant negative self talk can also cause them. No matter what age you are, your fears of public speaking don't seem to be related to whether you are a teenager or an adult. If you are constantly discouraged or make yourself feel bad, you may be putting yourself at risk for public speaking anxiety. People who make it a habit of thinking they'll fail, or that their speeches will be forgotten, are more likely not to succeed at public speaking.

Chapter 4: The Physiology And Public Speaking

In my particular case I found great comfort in understanding the neurobiological processes behind my fear. I found comfort in knowing that I was feeling a certain way because of a range common brain processes. Now, whenever I experience anxiety, regardless of the reason, I whisper in my head "Ahh, there is my Amygdala tagging some thing as fearful." Some people feel their anxiety, fear, and panic makes them "crazy", putting them at risk of some unknown process. It can be very useful to have an understanding of the "underside" of things. I will thus devote some space to explain exactly what's happening in your head when it comes to public speaking.

If an alien visited Earth and you told them (or it) that 75% experience fear while speaking to other humans, the alien will (perhaps very rightly) assume humans are insane. The alien would probably be correct to a certain extent. If you stop and think about it, the idea of speaking in front or to strangers would make you panic (as you are under attack) is absurd.

This is a great way of illustrating the sheer lunacy and fear. I am a social person and can communicate with people. I'm a social person and am comfortable talking to large groups at work. I would be fine explaining a topic to strangers or co-workers if I was asked. I would feel no anxiety if you added another person so that the topic or concept could be explained to two people. My brain would sense that I had moved beyond just talking to people to being able to present to a group. My brain suddenly thought it was in danger, at some undetermined point.

Another aspect to my own insanity was the amount of notice that I was given prior to being required. One particular instance is an excellent example. I was doing my work in an office when I noticed a senior executive of the company where I worked, and asked me to enter the room. I walked into the room, and I found my entire senior leadership team standing in front me. They asked me to tell them about a research project I'd been working on without much notice. Since my brain was not equipped to deal with this sudden speaking engagement, my brain just went into overdrive and I felt minimal anxiety. If the presentation had been requested more than a few weeks before, I would have suffered a week-long depression and even near-petrification in those days.

We'll say it again: Anxiety can seem like a strange beast.

Thierry Stimer describes anxiety so well in The Biology of Fear and Anxiety Related Behaviors.

Anxiety is a psychological and physiological state in which there is a potential threat to survival or well-being. It is characterized as increased arousal or expectancy, autonomic, neuroendocrine activation, and specific behaviour patterns.

If we were to cut through the brain to identify the source of this strange behaviour, we would discover the primary (but certainly not the only) culprit deep in the temporal cortex. This is the amygdala. Or amygdalae. It's an organ with an almond shape, or more precisely, a cluster (or nuclei) that is responsible for this behavior. The amygdala may be known as your "fear-centre", although this can be misleading. This could mean that the amygdala doesn't only have to do with fear or negative emotions. Although the amygdala triggers your fear reaction, it's also an essential part of your brain. It is also responsible for life's colour and emotion. The amygdala helps you attach emotional significance to events. People with impaired amygdala function as a result of brain injury or other causes live without emotion. It is an awful existence. It appears that in exchange for emotional joy, we also have to be able to feel anxiety and other negative emotions.

The reason why the amygdala is acting illogically, according to neuroscientists, is because the amygdala acts quickly and dirty. This is most evident in the well-known snake/rope example.

Imagine you are walking in the forest, or jungle, and suddenly you see a coiling object on the ground. Usually, what happens is you will jump back and feel stress hormones coursing through the veins. A few seconds later, you realize it was not a snake but a coil of rope. This can be attributed largely to your friend, the amygdala.

What just happened is that your amygdala based its very poor, low-resolution information has made a snap judgment. Your amygdala literally declares "I don't know whether this is a serpent or an innocuous, snake-like object. However, to be safe, I am going start panic stations." This is the reason this is called "quick, dirty". It bypasses all logic and reasoning and hijacks your body and brain using very rough information. Your brain's relay station has received the signal, which has sent it from your eyes and arrived at your conscious brain. This is when your brain's logical part, using a hi-resolution image taken from your eyes, determines that you see a piece of rope.

So why is the amygdala prone to overreacting? Because overactive amygdalas have kept everyone safe over the course and evolution of your ancestors. A hyperactive amygdala is a cause of many false alarms. It can also make it difficult to sleep at night. However, it would be a quick way to thin out your gene bank. The costs of panicking when you see coiled ropes or snake-shaped vines are low, but the risks of jumping back fast when there is actually a deadly serpent can be high.

The general principle of how the amygdala works is that there's a particular event that the amygdala marks as important. The amygdala worked in a remarkable experiment years ago. This experiment, aside from the fact it sounds a little cruel, was quite effective.

This experiment was carried out on a person with severe memory loss. The patient couldn't recall anything. A researcher could then enter the room, introduce themselves to the person, and then leave. The poor lady would lose all memories of ever having met with the researcher. The researcher did something very interesting. They placed a small pencil in each other's palm so that when they were shaking hands, the pin gave off a tiny prick to her hand. It caused her hand and wrist to relax. The researcher continued this process several more times. Then something incredible happened. Despite the fact she couldn't remember the researcher's name, the researcher eventually offered to shake hands. However, the lady declined. Because, even though her memory was impaired, her amygdala had the ability of identifying certain events and tagged them as significant. The amygdala finally realized that it was possible to be dangerous by shaking hands.

This is one of the most common problems with amygdalas, as well as the reason for virtually every possible phobia. First, the amygdala sometimes makes mistakes, labeling something as potentially dangerous when it is actually quite innocuous. This can lead the amygdala to make illogical phobias, such as fearful public speaking or fear of heights. While you may not be in actual danger, it can still cause severe anxiety. It can also be very time-consuming and difficult to extinguish fear when the amygdala has already decided. Exposure therapy is so slow because it takes so long for it to work. Consider that you are afraid to encounter snakes. First, visualize the snake. Then, look at photos and videos. Finally, take a look at real snakes in zoos. The stages may take several months in severe cases. You are basically trying to convince amygdala gradually that snakes pose no threat.

While the amygdala plays the most important role in public speaking anxiety, this is only one part of the brain. It is actually a complicated network of connections that your brain activates when you present to people. Norepinephrine is the neurotransmitter chief that sends messages across this network when you are feeling stressed or excited.

This network's main sub-group is called the hypothalamic Pituitary Adrenal axis (HPA Axis). If you are physiologically activated by a stimulus that causes stress, this axis transmits a message. It involves the release cortisol and adrenaline to prepare you for fight/flight. Your body prepares you to run quickly (by releasing blood glucose or fatty acids as energy) and to heal itself (by speeding up the inflammatory processes).

Another brain area, known as locus ceruleus (sometimes called coeruleus), is involved in fear and panic responses. Your brain's largest factory for norepinephrine, the locus Ceruleus, is located in your brain. Your brain releases norepinephrine when it is exposed to fear-provoking stimuli. The activity of drugs like barbiturates or benzodiazepines is reduced to a certain extent by increasing levels GABA, which reduces the activity of your locus Ceruleus.

Apologies for boreing you with neuroscience. I believe it is essential to understand what is happening on a biological level. Your reaction when you speak in public is not uncommon. Your reaction to public speaking is not unique. This biological process in your brain is caused by fear structures from the past over which you have limited control.

Chapter 5: Analyzing Your Audience

Understanding your audience's needs and wants is key to effective speech. It is much easier to communicate effectively with your audience if you are able to understand why they are there and what they expect from you. Think about it. A speaker's speech is something you anticipate hearing. This is the most valuable thing a speaker could do before they start speaking.

But how can we find out what the audience wants and needs? Two methods can be used to assess the needs of your target audience. These are the two main methods to analyze your audience's needs.

Demographic Analysis

Situational Analysis

Effective communication requires you to understand your audience. Audience analysis gives valuable insight about your audience. This can help to choose and develop relevant topics. In order for a message to resonate, it must be in tune with the audience's beliefs, values and opinions. It must also be in language the audience can understand and convey a message that interests them.

The demographics and the context of your topic are the two most important areas to analyze when you're analyzing your audience. A set of questions can be answered for each of the areas to stimulate your thinking about audience. The questions above should not be the only ones you answer. You also need to consider how each factor (age, socio-economic standing, etc.) influences your audience. You influence the opinions and attitudes of your audience.

Demographic Analysis

What is the audience like? Is my audience homogeneous? What are the commonalities between them? How are readers different if they're heterogeneous? What do readers have in Common despite their differences and how can they be matched?

What is my average age? What is the range of ages represented?

How would I describe my audience's socio-economic situation? They fit where?

What occupations do you see in my readers audience?

What are my readers' religious and political beliefs?

What are the cultural and ethnic groups represented in my readers audience?

What is my relationship with my reader audience? Are we in the same status or are we different?

Situational Analysis

What is my audience's knowledge of my topic?

What can I tell my readers about information they don't know? What new information could my readers be able to benefit? How can they make use of this information?

What time of the day will I be speaking to you?

Where will you be speaking?

Is the space suitable for the audience's comfort?

Are audience members required or allowed to attend?

What do they want to see from my speech?"

You might wonder what you can do before your speech to get to know your audience. In a classroom setting you are likely familiar with your audience because you've been to class with them. You should ask your audience members if they invite you to speak to them. Ask questions about their ages. Their gender. What knowledge they have about the topic. Why are they here? Are they looking for something in return or are they more interested in you being entertaining? Are you okay if your speech uses a persuasive approach? Will that make your audience uncomfortable? These are questions that your audience should be asking.

Once you have an idea of who your audience is, you can get to work organizing your speech. For organizing your speech, it is helpful to ask:

What is the general purpose (inform, persuade. entertain. celebrate) of my speech

What is the specific purpose or message of my speech?

Audiences are attracted to feeling like they've gotten their money's value. Offer your audience a benefit when you write your purpose. The following is an example of a specific purpose.

After listening today to my speech, you'll be well-informed about Cape May, New Jersey history.

Another example:

You will be convinced, after listening to my speech today, that you will choose a vegetarian diet.

What is the central idea/the thesis of my speech. This is how I see this topic.

Perhaps your goal is to persuade the audience to go vegetarian. Your central idea or thesis states that your audience will feel happier and healthier by becoming vegetarian.

Although we cannot view the minds of our audiences to determine what they want as speakers, there is a way to learn about them. These include:

Asking the person who invited and inviting you to speak

Before you go, conduct a survey of the audience

Pre-planning your speech venue

Make sure to research!

A speaker should choose message strategies to appeal to an audience's beliefs and opinions. The audience will perceive you differently and be able to understand your message if you take the time to get to know them.

Auditor Analysis Exercise

Imagine you're giving a speech highlighting the benefits and advantages of physical exercise.

You have the option to choose from several audiences.

Preschool

Middle School

High School

Collegiate Age

Senior Citizens

Pick one audience, and then write an introduction that is geared towards what you believe the audience needs.

You can share it with the class!

Chapter 6: The Structure and Outline For A Great Speech

A great speech seems effortless, captures attention and is filled full of information, great stories and fun jokes. A great speech only comes out of the practice and preparation that went into it. This book will show how to craft and deliver great speeches. It all starts with the structure of your speech.

The introduction is probably the most important portion of your speech. This set the tone for the entire speech and gives the audience a first impression. Great openings will draw their attention and get them excited to hear the rest. The chapter that follows will provide some excellent ideas for openings. This is something to keep in mind while you are writing your speech.

Next, start to prepare the body of your speech. The outline should be a description of the content of your speech.

What are the key points you want your audience understand? You can start by writing down these points. Next, you should list examples, quotes, or stories that support your argument. The type of speech you give will impact how persuasive or informative it is. In order to keep your audience engaged and awake, it is important to use jokes and stories in your speech. If they are given too much dull, boring information, they will lose attention and begin to daydream.

Once you have determined your main points and brainstormed stories and examples, you need to write a conclusion. What do you want the audience's final thoughts to be after the speech is finished? What is the final main thought that you want to instill in your audience after your speech? These questions should be considered as you create your conclusion. The conclusion should briefly review your 3 main points. It is important to keep it short. This is not an extension of your speech.

Then, finish with a memorable story or quote for them. You can also create your own closings, which will thank your audience for listening and reflect your purpose and vision. To make your speech unique and distinguish yourself as a speaker, you might consider creating a closing you can use in each speech. Robert H. Schuller adopted this phrase and it has been widely used today. You might think of a philosophy or motto that you would like to spread and incorporate this into the speech.

To deliver a great speech, you must put in the effort and work hard. When you have spent the time to prepare, such as creating an outline, introduction body, body, and conclusion for your speech, the first step towards delivering a great talk is complete.

Chapter 7: Generating Interest

This is the most important lesson I want to impart from this book. One of the most important goals that you should keep in mind when speaking is getting the audience's attention. As they listen, increase their interest in your speech.

Warren Buffett was a famous billionaire investor who once stated that his number one rule in investing is to "never let your shareholders lose their money" and his number two rule to public speaking was to "refer back to rule number one." However, instead of dealing on money, we are dealing here with the attention or interest of our audience.

When it comes down to public speaking, the key is to keep your audience's attention. If you lose your audience's attention, you will have a difficult time with the rest of your speech. Unless you say something really interesting, Sometimes it takes just twenty seconds to bore someone listening to your speech.

You have never seen someone so excite an audience that they end up doing terrible overall. No!

How can you get interest? Today, I will only briefly mention a few. One way to challenge your audience is to do so in a non-hostile fashion. If everyone in an audience thinks that pink brownies are the best, you can then explain to them why they taste better. While you could be hostile to the audience, this is a more advanced tactic.

One way to attract interest is to really know your subject. The more knowledgeable you are on a topic, generally speaking, the better your performance. When in doubt about your public speaking abilities, you should stick to what is most important. I cover more detail about how to generate curiosity in the other parts.

Avoid these words

An additional sign of an amateur speaker's inexperience is their tendency to use the words "uh" (or "um") too often. These types of filler words are detrimental to your speech and make the audience less likely to take your speech seriously. These words are best avoided by slowing down the speed of your talk so that you are aware of when and where you will be using them. It's fine to use filler words in every paragraph. However, if you do choose to use them in your speech, it is best to do so as sparingly and as minimally as possible. A great speech can be compared to a wonderful meal. It requires you to mix and match a range of elements. As an expensive dinner should have at least a portion of all the ingredients, a great speech also needs some nonsense to make its appeal more compelling. How great would a meal look if there was absolutely no fat in the meats used? Public speaking is no different.

Other words to avoid are large, complex words that not many people will know. Avoid obscure, multi-syllable terms unless you are asked to use jargon for a particular field like medicine. This will avoid you coming across as pompous or arrogant to the public. This should be an easy tip to remember because you only need to reduce or even eliminate large portions of your speech. Don't give the impression you know more than your audience.

Never underestimate power of the audience

Audiences respond emotionally to great speakers for a reason. The audience tends to react like a crowd so capture their energy.

Logically, the audience can ignore you if you don't give an effective speech.

With all of this being said, I believe the reason that fear and anxiety about public speaking are so prevalent is that you are basically being examined as though you were being examined under a microscope, by tens of thousands, hundreds, even thousands of people.

Every little thing you do and every word that you say is being considered in the minds and hearts of your listeners. The audience's power is what I am trying to convey.

Because you are constantly being watched by so many people, I want you to consider how your attitude, personality and thoughts manifest in your voice, body language, posture, and movement on the stage. Engaging the audience is possible by moving back and forth across stage. But don't overdo it.

What I'm referring to is that audience members will be able to sense if you feel superior. If you are trying to be kind to an audience member, they'll feel it too. It's possible for the audience to feel pompous if your actions are not humble. If you can be humble and consider the best interests and best interests of your audience, you will see a significant improvement in results.

It is almost as if the audience has an uncanny ability to judge your personality differently than if it were done individually. They are almost able to read your mind just by watching your body language. While they may not have the ability to read your thoughts about favorite foods, they do have the ability to determine if or not you are a conceited or stuck-up person. Sometimes, if a speaker is really conceited they may not realize it. You may have been an audience member at a time when a speaker was clearly conceited. But you weren't able to give exact reasons. Or maybe you heard about a speaker who was very funny, but you could tell he or she was a good person. What I'm referring to is the inexplicable power of the audience in critiquing and judging someone's innermost being. Keep this in mind and don't underestimate its power.

While the audience is powerful, one flaw is common to all audiences. It is the fact that all audiences have a very small attention span. If an average person can focus on a topic for one to two hours, I would guess that the average audience can do the same. They have an average attention span between three and four seconds. To maintain the attention of the audience, it is crucial to keep them engaged throughout the speech. Once you get the audience's attention and keep it there for a few minutes, things will get easier. You have built a level in credibility and they will continue to listen to you even if your jokes and cleverness are great.

Chapter 8: Why Public Speaking?

Preface has answered a substantial portion of this question. Let me now share some additional, but still important, benefits to learning public speaking.

Public Speaking and Your Job

We can help you get the designation you desire

Many employees have been working at a job that is not up to their potential. Although they deserve a better title, many employees work in jobs that limit their opportunities to utilize their talents.

It is your presentation at a job interview which ultimately determines whether you will be offered a higher-paying role. Your employer will consider you the person they will turn to when they encounter difficult situations. Confident, confident speakers are a step above those who lack the ability to express themselves and are thus less impressive.

Clear and effective communication is the key to being at your best. You can achieve the best you have to offer by being a good public speaker. It is important to realize that the true value in the knowledge you have can only be realized when there are the right channels and ways to share your wisdom.

Public speaking is not only a great way to increase your knowledge as you prepare, but it also shows your confidence. Your enthusiasm is what will make it stand out in a crowd of other applicants, no matter if you are applying for a job. Don't be afraid to speak out and claim the job that you deserve.

Electrify your Presentations and Nail Your Board meetings

I had the pleasure of speaking to David, a senior manager. His name has been changed to protect anonymity. He spoke out about the difficulties of being at the same position for six years. Not only his colleagues but also his juniors had achieved higher salaries and received promotions. My further research revealed that he was a skilled manager, but not at his best in public speaking. As he sat in front of the projector or addressed his seniors, he would feel sweaty on his forehead. His hands and legs would tremble and, most often, he would end up falling between the cracks. Even though his presentations were among the best, his nervousness would sometimes make it difficult for him to deliver them. This made his senior clients and colleagues doubt his abilities. He was eventually promoted to backend operation.

This issue was so troubling that he thought he wasn't worthy of his job and decided to resign. However, he did not give up on his career nor his identity. He made one wise move. He decided to give it a last shot but this one time under the guidance a mentor. This lead to our meeting.

The first thing that I shared was an incident in the history of Swami Vivekananda. Swami Vivekananda was just

20 years old when he went to Varanasi in the Ganges River. This was shortly after Sri Ramakrishna died and before Swami Vivekananda went to America in 1893.

Swami visited many holy locations and met many notable scholars upon his arrival to Varanasi. A troop of monkeys attacked him while he was visiting Goddess Durga's Temple. Vivekananda ran away from the monk, who shouted, "Face those brutes!" Vivekananda stopped. The monk pointed out the beasts to him and they disappeared quickly.

Vivekananda took the incident to heart and used it in his talks in the United States.

He stated that "the ultimate goal" was to not enjoy life but to conquer the world. To do this, we must gain control of our fears and anxieties. Our mental makeup should be strong enough to prevail no matter what circumstances we may find ourselves in.

Vivekananda urged us to be brave and not fear. Fear is the leading cause of world-wide misery. Fear is the greatest superstition. Fear is the root of our woes. It is fearlessness that brings about heaven in a moment.

The next step was restoring David's confidence by using proven techniques. I made a plan and asked him for guidance to get through the difficult times. After three months, his boss offered him the chance to speak at top-notch clients' presentation. The presentation was planned for the following week. David was not at ease with his boss, but he was determined to give him the final ten-minute slot. David took advantage of this opportunity to regain and increase his confidence.

His presentation was a success. It increased the company's customer base as well as earning him the title Senior Sales Manager. After another eight months, I received a phone call from him to inform that he had been appointed Sales Head.

David's tale is only a glimpse into how public speaking can empower you to be a competent broadcaster. With your excellent public speaking skills you can make a lasting impression upon your seniors. This communicates to the company that you are a skilled and dedicated employee. It is possible that you will be the first candidate to be recommended for a senior job vacancy.

Public speaking is a highly prized skill, whether it's at the podium or in board meeting meetings.

A member can present a nine-minute business pitch at every Tajurba gathering. This is an important day for members as they get to showcase their business to the entire group. One time, a graphics designer was presenting the business. He was nervous, and didn't do his homework properly. His PowerPoint didn't work during his presentation. He was very nervous and fumbled a lot. Even though he was a brilliant graphic designer, everyone thought he wasn't knowledgeable about his business. He stopped getting referrals. He quit Tajurba membership.

Display Your Leadership Skills

Public speaking allows you to display your leadership skills. Your leadership skills may be well-known, but your ability to influence others at a higher level could make you an unknown hero. You may be able influence your colleagues or teammates. Perhaps you have the natural ability to make your point and show your sincerity to your company. However, there might be something that is holding you back; fear of being on stage.

You can't be a leader without followers. Leaders are able to inspire and persuade others, and they can do that by communicating well. Leaders need to know how communicate their ideas and get people to take notice. If you consider yourself a leader for the future, public speaking should be a core skill.

Speaking publicly improves your leadership skills. This will make you a more desirable candidate to be successful in your chosen field. Bill Gates once declared, "As the next century approaches, leaders will be those people who will empower others."

Public Speaking and Your Business

Fundraising that Converts

I have seen many startups hold pitching sessions and witnessed poor startups receive funding as the founder was a skilled presenter. On the flip side, I have also witnessed great businesses get denied funding because the founder didn't know how to present their business in front investors.

Recently, I met a billionaire businessman. He has been active in his chosen area for the last 30 years. He is proud to be a millionaire. But he wasn't content. His dilemma was that his uncle's child and he both started at the exact same time with the same investment. They also had the same product. Both were qualified with the same background. His uncle's brother was five times as wealthy as this gentleman. They were still good friends but this vast difference worried him.

Further research revealed that his uncle's son was involved with the business deals. Instead of having his sales representative approach the clients, he would instead take the initiative. He prepared the presentation slides himself, which helped his clients feel more confident. This also increased their funding and consequently the gains. Additionally, he communicated with his staff often and resolved their problems direct rather than passing responsibility to HR or his manager. This helped employees feel valued and made them feel more invested in their organization.

This gentleman was not like his cousin and was afraid to meet clients. He said to me, "If I can do everything myself then why do you need to hire qualified staff?" Despite knowing this, he was still afraid. After only a few more minutes, he was ready to sign up for my public speaking program. He smiled as he said, "This has been something I've been running from for years. I think it is time to finally take the bull by his horns."

He met me after a while and, with an ear-to ear-smile, said that "Public speaking does matter!" I'm able not only to get more investors but also the environment at work has drastically changed. Your employees are more energetic and therefore more productive. You have revolutionized our business!"

Do PR like a pro

Public speaking adds an extra dimension to your confidence. Public speaking can be a way to ensure smooth sailing, whether that's at events or in leading PR campaigns. You don't have to worry about making mistakes or falling on your face when faced with difficult situations. It takes practice to discover the best ways you can communicate your vision about the company. Even if you're asked unanticipated queries, you won't lose heart. You will be able manage any situation with the same finesse as a pro.

Our company was changed from Public Limited to Public Limited. It was listed on stock exchange. In 1995, our merchant banker organized press conferences for all the major Indian cities. I had to participate in many interviews and give many speeches at these conferences. All the cities received a high rating from the press. They rated them as excellent. The company's core principles were the key to its success. My presentations were also well received by the media.

However, I should add that handling public relations to raise your public awareness does more than just delivering your sales pitch on the stage or table. You should provide something of value for your targeted audience. This should be both educative and informative. This type of speaking is beneficial for many reasons:

* It declares that you are an expert in your chosen subject. You become the resource. People like to buy from experts.

* If you manage PR, you are always in a giving mood. You communicate information, tips techniques, methods, ideas, and other useful information. Maybe you share some real-life stories that your audience can relate to. This will make your audience feel valued.

* Your costs are low. It is better to send your message one time to everyone than many times to every prospect.

* You build a trusting relationship by giving people a way to communicate with each other. Many people will want you to communicate with them after you have spoken.

After your presentation, you develop a convertible list of highly targeted prospects to market to. You are more likely for these targeted, interested audiences to buy from than anyone with a small presence. They would prefer to be connected to someone they have heard, over someone they don't know.

Create Growth Opportunities

You may want to grow and reach new heights, but not like a frog from the well. Here, I believe practice is the key. The more you practice this skill, the easier it will be to persuade others. These leaders inspire confidence and enthusiasm. This reminds us of the great personalities Azimpremji and Ratan Tata. I have met many Tata/Wipro employees that love their company and wish to retire from the company. They regard their work as their passion and idolize them. However, investors are more likely to invest in such exceptional personalities than they are in their work. This not only helps to expand the company's reach but also increases its potential supporters.

Your Voice Can Make a Difference

Speaking is the best way to fulfill all your aspirations and needs. Public speaking is the way to go, whether you want to be a successful businessman, parent or coach. You are able to inspire others and make their lives happier. These achievements are enough to make you want to master this skill.

Communication is the key to bridging the gap between you, your goals and everything else.

Great leaders have inspired us with their words more than their actions.

Many of us are not using our voices to the fullest extent. You're not here for a dull existence, but to make the most of your voice.

It is time to "discover you own voice."

Speaking is the best way to fulfill your greatest desires and needs as a human being.

Once you learn the power of the voice, you will realize the enormous responsibility that comes along with it. You can build walls. Or you can build bridges. It's up to you.

My words and their impact on others are my responsibility whenever I speak. I am responsible for whether my words encourage positive thinking and inspire others or if they fall on deaf ears.

Super leaders accept responsibility for the words that they speak. Their words have impact. This is what we call the "next level" of leadership. Simply put: there should be conviction, and accountability in your words. Your convict and your convenience don't share the same block. Your conviction and purpose for living are two different things. Do you desire to live your whole life as a leader? Or a follower? Your voice can be uplifting. You can offer strength and hope to the powerless.

Make a difference in the lives and livelihoods of others by forming your voice

Our voice can either be used as a way to motivate people or to bring them down. It all boils down to how we communicate our message to make people happy. Many speakers have made an impact by using the power of speech to destroy or attack humanity. Hitler used his ability to speak to inflict havoc on humanity, while Nelson Mandela used this same power to protect the rights of his fellow citizens in a peaceful but effective manner. Although both may be remembered today by many, what is important is who among them is most loved by the masses.

Consider asking yourself these questions: How can I be of value to anyone I meet, whether they are waiters at a restaurant table or the CEO and president of a company?

To be open to seeing everyone, you must not be prejudiced. You also need to be authentic in your voice. This brings us onto the next aspect.

Be authentic in the voice you use

Consider what it would be like if you had nothing to defend, to prove, or to hide.

What would it feel like to be able to live from that place today. Primarily, being authentic means marking your presence. It is aligning with the best of yourself, no matter if you are speaking in front one person or one thousand people or in private when no one is watching. You don't need to be ashamed or protected.

The power of face-to-face contact is a powerful motivator. It allows people to see your knowledge and wisdom, that you live up to your promises and that you are passionate about the product and service you provide. This allows them to see themselves working together. This will allow you to generate high-quality leads and not rely on other channels such as Google ads or Facebook. However, these platforms can be very important. Public speaking events, however, simply provide the foundation for deeper connections at a faster rate.

The compelling reason behind anything you do in life is crucial. This serves as a motivator. In the final chapters of this book you will learn about the mechanics of public speech. But before that you must be as fluent in public speaking as you are with breathing. Let's look at public speaking as an option for a career.

Chapter 9: The Nature Of The Beast: Public Speaking and Stage Fright

Let's get started. I'm no random guy from the street. I've been to stage before, many times, from elementary to highschool, so stage fright is an old phobia of mine.

I've given a few speeches. All of them were done spontaneously. I've never prepared a speech in advance. I can tell you that I do know what I am talking about in terms of this.

Let's first define the term "public speaking". Let's take a look at some definitions found on the internet and come up with the following:

Public speaking involves the giving of speeches, often to large numbers of people, for information, entertainment or persuasion.

It is also ranked highly in a few studies regarding what people fear. It seems quite bizarre, considering it only requires getting up, talking with a few people, then sitting back down.

While it's not easy, the bottom line is that it's not. It is strange how a seemingly simple thing can make jelly out the knees so many. The fear is not unfounded. However, this fear is mostly caused by stage fright.

The fear is manifested in the numerous fears that surround the potential public speaker. He may be afraid of making a fool out of himself and making a big mistake in front.

You might also doubt your ability to deliver a quality performance. A speaker might feel pressured or be embarrassed by the idea of putting on a good performance. The speaker may also be concerned about her appearance.

These are valid concerns. One of the most bizarre things about public speaking in public is that it is all too familiar. Unless there is a special circumstance, most people who speak publicly also speak every day to a few people.

The problem lies when a familiar thing is dropped into an unfamiliar environment. Instead speaking to one or two people about anything pertinent that comes to their minds, one speaks with a large number of people about a particular subject about which the speaker may have no knowledge.

It is possible that the audience might not know what to do. In some cases this could be beneficial. A non-speaking audience may not recognize the speaker's nervousness cues and mistakenly pass them off.

In many cases, the unfamiliarity of the audience can be a disadvantage to the speaker. This is because the speaker doesn't know them and may feel awkward and less comfortable. Even worse, social differences could lead to self-consciousness. If the whole audience is dressed in white tie, it can make it very difficult to deliver speeches.

The reason you are so scared is that there is nothing between the speaker of the performance and the audience.

The speaker is not acting (deliberately), or playing any instrument. Instead, he is only using his voice, with or minus the assistance of microphones.

The speaker is responsible for any mistakes made during the speech, unless the equipment fails. With little else to shift the burden to, the speaker bears all of this responsibility.

The level of fright depends on many things. The audience is an important factor. Some people do better with audiences that number more than a thousand and others turn into jelly when they have only twenty.

Some individuals may be more comfortable with people from different social groups than others and less comfortable speaking to their peers. Other people might find it more difficult to make friends with close friends than with random acquaintances or others. Some environments may cause more fear than others.

There are many other possible factors that can cause fear, too many to list here, but the ones listed above are usually the main ones.

Chapter 10: Wear your heart on the sleeves

It is not necessary to reveal information about you that is very personal or difficult to share. This wouldn't be appropriate nor beneficial.

This principle isn't about boring your audience with every little detail about your life.

There have been times when, while giving a speech I felt like I was expressing myself in a different way to my previous speeches.

Your heart isn't about trying to look genuine, warm or sincere. It is about being genuine, kind, warm and sincere.

In an impromptu talk about work and employers, for example, I found myself describing a group former colleagues as being like family. As a result, the decision to leave this job was one I regret most. I confessed that I meant what I said and believed it to be true. This was despite not having ever told the group of ex-colleagues this in as many words. This detail had not been revealed to me when I started my speech. I was just trying my best to deliver the speech as honest and heartfelt as possible.

The section on treating others as you would treat them addressed the importance and necessity of speaking off-the cuff. This is similar to the idea that you should always wear your heart on the sleeve, which is why many sections in this book are interrelated. This can signify that what you say is more in line with your thoughts and feelings at the specific moment, and therefore may be more authentic.

While this is not to imply that all speeches should be prepared, it does mean that some portions of a talk may benefit from being delivered impromptu. Even if a speaker is careful to provide enough detail that it aligns with the purpose of the talk, it is not enough if the details are not consistent with their belief at the moment.

Although it is possible for a speaker to present stories or details that are not true, some members of the audience might be suspicious and feel less inclined or able to listen.

Openness and honesty are two of the most powerful things a speaker can do in order to connect to their audience.

Chapter 11: The First Honey

John bear witness of him and cries, saying, This is the man of whom he spoke. He that follows me is preferred above me because he was my predecessor. All that we received was from him in all his fullness, as well as grace for grace.

John 1:15-16

There's always a first honey to every situation in life.

John the Baptist had already prepared the way to Christ before Christ was made public. John the Baptist, Christ's first honey attracted and pointed people towards the Savior.

John the Baptist was the voice of John the Baptist crying in wilderness. This is what the Bible refers to. "Then they spoke unto him, "Who art thou?" We can give an answer for them who sent. What would you say of yourself? He said, "I'm the voice of one crying out in the wilderness. Follow the Lord's lead, as Esaias stated" (John 1, 22-23).

The First Attraction

If you're married, you can think of those first times you saw your spouse or the first thing about her that got you interested in her. You may fall in love and be a complete stranger to her.

What was it exactly? Are you attracted to her only for the sake or attraction? No! But there was more to her than that. Her beauty was captivating and it made you want to be closer.

Perhaps she's beautiful and radiant, and you were drawn to her. Or perhaps she doesn't really care what you think about her. Maybe that was because she didn't know you wanted to be with her.

Perhaps she's a melody you like. Maybe she moves like dancing music.

Perhaps her singularly fresh and beautiful eyes are due to her stunning beauty and honesty. Or she may walk like an angel during a fashion parade.

Or perhaps her smile was flirtatious but sociable. Maybe all things about her were triumphantly elegant.

You were attracted to this woman regardless of the reasons. She is a real rockstar or a complete savior! I'm talking about how she got into your heart! It was her first kiss that attracted your attention.

So what's my point? Simply put: Your public ads will be the first honey to attract people to your speaking event.

It is easier to catch fly with honey than vinegar. It is because people think they are poor that big companies will continue making large amounts of money.

It is very unfortunate that this happens, even though it is a sad truth.

It's easy to see how this works. What do you think the majority of average companies do in order to make huge profits on the common man's money? Do they give you vinegar as an alternative to water? Maybe.

Or maybe it's just because you know them enough as a well-respected, successful, and reliable company that delivers what they promise. You may be right.

Or because?. . because . . . because . . . They might offer honey instead vinegar.

Yes, yes, indeed!

You get it at a very high price! They know what they want! They know what you want, and you often do it! You'll often end up paying for it. And you often get yourself broke and in debt! You often make them richer!

This is something that the telecommunications and media industries are extremely skilled at. You can learn from them.

To attract the flies, you need to know how to serve honey as an alternative to vinegar. So what's the honey? The honey is their real desire for the event you're organizing; or what benefits you claim to have.

Proclaim Your Claim & Offer What You Preach

Now think about the moment you met your spouse. Did you give her honey or vinegar? Did you not appreciate her beauty and praise it? Didn't it feel good to say all that you could, when you had the opportunity?

Is it possible that you have become a poet for her and her love, and spoke so romantically about her? You checked on her every day, was your voice not soft, milky, and supple each time?

Yes

Your speaking business should be the same. Don't be afraid to give your audience honey.

For example, they might see your flyer, How You Can Make $1,500+ Monthly Working at Home. They are really looking for $1,500+ and the freedom to do so from their home. Or, simply put, without any hassle.

Why?

Because they are interested in a new car and an apartment that overlooks Aso Rock, they plan to show off their new wealth to their neighbors. They will put on intimidating regalia and latest designer clothes to lead a shining lifestyle that is like a super star.

If you understand what they want at your seminar, then you should be able to guide them in the right direction.

It is important to understand and get to know your audience's mindset. Next, tell them about the benefits of attending your speaking event by sharing what knowledge you have and/or enjoy doing.

Your public ad serves as your invitation to your audience. This should offer some benefits. Inform your audience about what they will gain by attending your presentation.

The importance of planning your publicity, which is an integral part your speaking business, cannot be underemphasized. It should include the topic or topics to be discussed, time, date and venue.

If you feel that there are others you would love for to grace the occasion, you could also send them a personal invitation.

Chapter 12: Overcoming Obstacles

I. I.

Mannerisms, or gestures you use to deliver your speech, are actions that you either intend or not to do.

Even though you may not notice, your audience may notice that you touch your nose and fix your clothes while you're on stage.

If possible, avoid these mannerisms.

1. Touching your nose/mouth.

2.Repair your dress even if the original is in good condition.

3.Looking towards the ceiling or onto the floor

4. Fixing your hair.

5. Roll your eyes.

6. Rolling the Microphone's wire (for wired microphones)

Your entire performance is visible from the stage. Avoid distracting your audience.

Remember that you're there to make your point and convince them of what you have to offer.

You should use less to deliver your speech. You don't need to be doing as many things as you do acting or dancing. But, you are a speaker and not an actor.

II. WHAT TO DO WHEN YOU FORGET YOUR

LINE?

You're about to give your speech. Then suddenly, something clicked in your head that was completely off-topic.

What should you now do?

Are you going back to the backstage crying because your speech is not over?

Many did just that. People started cheering, and they forgot their lines.

I don't want you experiencing this. It's a really bad feeling. It can even lead to depression. You may eventually become averse to public speaking.

I want you to be a confident public speaker.

So, here are some guidelines.

Here are some tips for when you get stuck in the middle of a speech and forget what to say.

You can take a break for a minute...

If you are on the podium or at the lectern, get up.

Move a little on stage

Try to recall your training and rehearsals while you are walking so you can recall the lines and words you remembered.

Make eye contact and keep your eyes open to the audience.

Try to walk back a little to find the last word you wanted to say.

You should have at this point remembered your word.

Bring yourself back to the original position and continue speaking with courage.

Finish it with power

After walking backwards and forth, but still not remembering anything, you were completely confused. Here are your options.

Do not worry about your speech, instead talk about the subject in your own words.

For a continuation of your previous work, send an IMPROMPTU SPECH.

Sometimes the best speech is spontaneous, because it just comes out of your mouth. No fancy words. Use your everyday words.

End your speech, and say thanks.

At this moment, the audience is standing and giving the most applause possible to the person who lost his speech but still managed to finish it.

You'll feel vindicated.

Never apologize to your audience. Public speaking is not the time for an apology. Stand up for your rights and be a man.

III. HOW TO COMPETE WITH NERVES

Some people are nervous about giving their speeches because they fear the following: Audience and subject matter, venue set up, preparation and self-esteem.

Following my practical guidelines is the best way to deal with nerves.

It is important to research your audience in advance before you start your speech.

Scenarios

If you are already in class and you know everyone, that is a good thing. Follow the other steps.

When speaking to an unfamiliar audience, ensure you arrive on time and attempt to discover who they are. This will help with your introduction, delivery, handling of them and the rest.

Make sure you know your audience and your competitors before entering a speech competition.

Sometimes judges or cameras can be very intimidating. However, don't let that stop you from focusing on your speech delivery.

Make sure you're a master of the subject matter you choose, and that your heart is open to new ideas.

Mastery can be the best remedy.

Keep your copy aside before you deliver your speech.

If you feel butterflies around your stomach, this is normal. As long your subject matter is well-known, you can relax and remain calm.

If you don't have any idea about the location or how it's set-up, it might be worth going to visit it.

If you can, practice at the venue. Step on the stage to feel the atmosphere.

Examine the physical structure of your venue. This will help you to decide where judges, VIPs, as well as other important people, will be sitting.

Doing this will make you more ready to go when you stand up on stage. You will also be better equipped to engage your audience as you deliver your message.

Preparation is the best preparation.

Do the following:

Prepare your PowerPoint Presentation before you start.

Don't forget to bring some towel or tissue if you don't have any other materials. You will definitely need this, believe me.

Believe in your ability to do it. If you don't believe in yourself, it will lead to a lot more troubles and a loss of success.

Believe that you can do it.

Do not harbor negative thoughts. Stay positive.

These guidelines will help overcome your fear of the stage and keep you calm. It is easy to follow and it will work.

Chapter 13: How To Deliver A Speech

Monore's motivational sequence

It is never easy to give a public speech. The reason is that every time you deliver your public speech, you are faced with a new audience and must adapt to their circumstances. It doesn't matter what topic you are presenting, it is important that you follow a common sequence when delivering your speech. Monore's Motivational Sequence is an example of such a universal sequence. To give an effective speech, the speaker needs to be involved with the audience through a series. These sequences could be:

Attention

No Need

Satisfaction

Visualization

Action

Attention

An effective speech starts with the speaker grabbing the attention of the audience. For this purpose, you can begin your speech telling a story, making predictions, sharing shocking statistics, pictures, videos or any other information.

No Need

Once you have their attention, it is now your turn to show them why the topic of this speech is important. Let them convince others that they should listen to your topic.

Satisfaction

The purpose of your speech is to explain the solutions. Your approach must be clear, specific, straight-forward, and easy to understand by the audience. Your best effort should be given to convince them that you have the best solution and also the most efficient. Your own personal experience and examples can be used to support your solution.

Visualization

The next step is to present the audience with the final results of the solutions that you provided. If they reject your ideas, then this step will be completed. There are two possible approaches to this. Positive is the way you tell your audience what they can do to make it more likely that they will follow the advice. The negative method is when you present the reasons that people may not be following your message. Each of these options can be used to enhance your speech. The best way to convince your audience of the benefits and draw them in is to compare the positive and negative aspects.

Action

Monore's sequence technique requires that the audience performs the last step. Your final, powerful statement should convince the audience to accept your solutions.

Presentation tips

Pronunciation

A lack of clarity in pronunciation of difficult words can cause speakers to fail to connect with the audience. Be patient and take the time necessary to correctly pronounce every word in your speech. Instead, try to avoid complicated words.

Anxiety control

Nearly all presenters experience anxiety before their speech. Increased self-confidence can help to reduce anxiety and provide knowledge on the topic. It is a good idea to take a few moments before your speech to make sure you are ready for the audience. It is very beneficial to take a deep inhale before you begin your speech.

First impression

Your first impression is what will make or break your entire presentation. You must dress in a professional manner with neat, clean clothes.

Postures

Proper posture is essential to a successful speech or presentation. Straighten your spine and face the audience. Your body weight should eventually spread throughout the time that you spend on the stage.

Gestures

Positive gestures will significantly improve your self-confidence while you are on stage. Do not feel embarrassed or anxious during your speech. Instead, take a few slow steps and relax.

Eye contact

It is possible to calm your nerves by keeping eye contact with the audience during your speech. It is important to make eye contact with your audience members from the beginning. When you are able to establish a connection, do not hesitate to speak with the person. When you've managed to get the attention of that person, you can then move to another person. It is important to keep the audience engaged throughout your speech by keeping their eyes open.

Avoid reading

It is important to not only refer to the slides, but also any visual aids. It is not recommended to be read out but used as a supplement to your message.

Expressions of the facial skin

Show your positive and positive feelings towards the topic or presentation. This is an essential tool for a good speech.

Avoid using filler words

The speech should not contain filler words like "um", "ah", or "you know". Instead, try to maintain silence while you practice your speech for the stage. This will enable you to avoid filler sentences completely on your final stage presentation.

Rehearsal

The best way to improve your skills is to practice. It is important to practice your speech and presentation repeatedly. You can present it to your friends or alone. Ask your friends for feedback. They can point out where you need more work. Also, it is crucial to do a full dress rehearsal prior to the final presentation.

Chapter 14: Build Confidence

You don't get born with an unlimited level of self-confidence. You can tell if someone has incredible self-confidence that they have been working hard to build it. You have to learn how to build self-confidence because it can be destroyed by the business world and life in general.

Here are some suggestions to help you build self-confidence in your role as a Speaker.

Identify yourself and Find Your Source for Shyness

Everyone experiences shyness differently. It is important to understand your own shyness and identify the situations that trigger it. You might feel uncomfortable speaking in public. Or, are you shy and nervous? When you are able identify yourself and understand the source of your shyness, then you can start to overcome it.

Start with very,very small talk and simple action:

Get your feet wet. People who are shy report having trouble communicating with people they just met, especially those to whom it is attracted. This strategy can help shy people overcome their insecurity. Start by starting with relatively non-threatening situations. It might be malls or museums, political rallies or sporting events that offer the chance to interact with many people for a short time. For such interactions, smile and say hello to as many people who are willing to make eye contact and give you a chance to be seen. There are three simple ways you can get used to talking to people: asking for directions, giving a compliment, and offering assistance (e.g. by holding a door). The goal is to become comfortable with talking with others.

How to continue talking while developing conversation skills

Shy people can improve their communication skills by learning how to make small talk. It is important to have something you can say to make a conversation successful. Shy people can use simple strategies to make sure they have something interesting to say. It is possible to start by reading or listening radio programs, as well as magazines. The advantage of such information sources is that they also give you the type of in-depth, "behind-the-headlines" analysis that is the basic substance of much social conversation. Shy people may also help to keep the conversation alive by asking open ended questions that demand more than a "yes or no" answer (e.g. . . ? ?

Be open to the idea of audience expressions

If you misinterpret an audience member's facial expression, it can increase your anxiety. Normal conversation is one in which we expect feedback from the listener. A nod and smile can indicate approval. Presenters listen to their audience differently. Their tendency to look blankly at speakers doesn't mean they don't enjoy what they hear. Rather, it means they are focused on the message.

This is especially true if the audience member is introverted.

Become an expert in your chosen topic

If you thoroughly research your topic, it will help increase your confidence in speaking publicly. The information that you share in your speech is only part of the entire topic knowledge. If you don't research the topic thoroughly, you will have anxiety about your speech.

Learn to Take Rejection: Everyone Is Not Liked.

Acceptance is part of social interactions. The key to conquering shyness is to not take rejection personally. There are many reasons why someone might be rejected by someone else. One person may not be able to stand the shy person's clothes, while another may become bored of the whole situation and not just her conversations with the shy person. You can control your reactions sometimes (e.g. wearing stylish clothes) and sometimes you cannot. What is important is that shy people are able to make realistic attempts at socializing with others.

Find Your Comfort Zone. Do What Feels Right.

Not all social situations are right for everyone. One example is that some people who are shy might not be comfortable in a nightclub, bar or club where physical attractiveness and stylish attire are crucial predictors for social success. You might also find success in situations where you have a lot of knowledge about politics, art, or mysteries. Shy people should search for the best matches to their temperaments and interests. It's easier for shy people find situations that make them feel comfortable. It is possible to volunteer at various organizations to help shy people feel more comfortable. Volunteering doesn't require much skill and allows for you to meet many different people. It is also easy to terminate if things don't go according to plan. To overcome shyness, it is possible to seek out volunteer opportunities in order to meet new people, improve social skills, and find the most comfortable situations.

Try to be the worst.

Although you may be familiar with your material, it is easy to get distracted when you are practicing a speech. Instead of actually thinking through what you are going say, you might just flip through the slides while you think about what to say. If you have 100 eyes looking at your presentation, it can cause you to lose focus and make your presentation less effective.

Focus on Your Message, Not on Your Fear

The more anxious you are about speaking, the greater your anxiety. Instead, think about your major ideas, introduction, conclusion, and time before you speak. Do not be afraid to focus on your ideas.

Visualize Your Success

Think about giving your speech. Picture yourself confidently walking to front and delivering the opening remarks. As confident and controlled as possible, you will give the entire speech. Imagine yourself as calm and in control.

You can practice breathing exercises

Proper breathing technique will help you have a confident, strong voice. You can project your voice well and speak with a relaxed tone by doing some basic exercises. Particularly useful for when you are speaking to a group.

Posture

For you to breathe properly, it is important that your posture allows for deep exhalation. Keep your feet close to shoulder width apart. Place your weight on the balls of both your feet and your heels. Every exhale will release tension in your shoulders, relax your neck and jaws, and allow your shoulders to relax.

Exaggerated Movement Exercise

Deep breathing is made easier when your throat and jaw are relaxed. Rosemary

Scott Vohs, a Western Washington University storytelling and speech communication instructor, suggests using exaggerated movements to open the throat and ease tension in the jaw. First, lift your eyebrows. Next, open your mouth wide. Next, yawn wide and loudly.

You should know the difference between your Introduction and Conclusion.

The ability to present your speech with confidence will help you calm your nerves and reduce anxiety. Your confidence will increase if your conclusion is clear, concise, and memorable. It will also help you to reduce nervousness during your speech. A good strategy to know the introduction and conclusion is to write them down word for word. Then, you can read them aloud to yourself a few more times. You can listen to their sounds and make any needed changes. Once you are satisfied, write them down. Although you don't want to memorize all of your speech, memorizing the introduction and conclusion will allow you to speak fluently without anxiety.

Chapter 15: Public Speaking Is Easy... It is All In Your Mind!

How can we define public speech? Public speaking is any speech made in public and not private, often to an audience that includes one or more people. You would define public speaking as a job interview. Yes.

One of my students shared her experience with me, saying that she was confident in her public speaking skills and that it helped her present herself well at interviews. A job interview is a public speaking occasion.

Learn the truth about public speaking.

Public Speaking is a mental process

Public speaking is an art form

Public Speaking is a habit

Public Speaking refers to a performance

Once you are able to understand the truths of public speaking, you will be able to address any fears or concerns you may have about this activity.

The mind holds all your faith, fear, and confidence. If your mind can become an effective speaker, it will overcome all of your fears.

Public Speaking requires mental skills

What thoughts run through your mind while you are preparing to deliver a speech.

Are you curious if the skills you possess are sufficient? Are you curious if speaking is something you can do? Are you wondering what errors you might make? Are you concerned about who will be watching? Are you worried you'll be boring? Are you worried about what you might look like?

These fears can cause nervousness, stomach butterflies, dry mouth and other symptoms in your body. If you have been following the exercises described in the earlier chapters, your worries and fears should dissipate.

You're ready to tackle the mind-bending tricks that your brain can play if vocabulary has been developed by reading widely and word gathering, if exercises have been performed regularly, and if it has been beneficial to your body through healthy eating and exercise.

A low level of fear will be avoided if you can understand your fears and make the effort to overcome them. You will feel anticipation, excitement, and exhilaration. But, you need to work hard.

Forget about 10 years ago. Or what happened 10 decades ago. Forget how someone made you feel. Forget about your past. A positive attitude is key to your success as a public speaker.

Visualize yourself as a successful presenter, especially since you have done all your work. I have not yet spoken about the topic of how to.

While you are writing your speech, it will take some time.

You already know lots about many things, but you think you don't because you aren't asked. This is a way to see how much you know about cheese. A 100-word speech can be written in your notebook. It doesn't need to be based on any research. It should take you 5-10 minutes. See what you come up. You'll see that your mind is open to any topic.

Public speaking can be a practice

Don't pass up the chance to speak publicly!

You may be at a conference and now it is time to have a question and answer session. Speak up at the microphone to ask a question. Do this at home privately so that you become familiar with your voice. Talk to someone you meet at a social function. Volunteer to read for children at a library, school or home - children don't mind being criticized!

If you have not been regularly practicing speaking in public on any topic, you will find it difficult to wait until that moment comes.

You'll find new ideas and opinions when you start reading more.

How prepared would it be to be interviewed for the media? Record yourself practicing; it could be a video recording, or an audio recording. This allows you to become familiar with how you sound to others and can adjust the tone of voice to suit your presentation.

Public Speaking is a habit

Making public speaking a daily practice is important. Get into the habit of doing everything you know to help you become a good speaker.

Do not let it slip for one day. You must practice every day to be able to play the guitars, violins or pianos.

Your public speaking habits should be developed. Set goals and keep them in your notebook. The chapters have provided you with tips. Do it!

Public Speaking refers to a performance

Keep in mind that public speaking a performance!

Public speaking is something that you are constantly doing. This means you must always perform to your best. It is vital that you have a positive mental attitude and practice it regularly to ensure you perform at the highest level. Although it will take some time to see the results, it is possible in as little two weeks. Your habits and practice will lead to dramatic improvements over time.

Chapter 16: Preliminary Notes For Your Speech

Before you begin to prepare for your speech there are some important factors you should be aware of.

What is your purpose

What is the purpose? What are you trying do? Are you trying persuade your co-workers to read your business plan or convince them to donate money to your favourite charity? Maybe you're trying to honour your brother and entertain his guests. This is a crucial step in preparing your speech. This is an important step. It's worth taking the time to clarify. It is a good idea for you to write your goal down so that it can be referred to often.

Who Is Your Audience

Your speech must resonate with your audience and satisfy their needs. A talk about rose gardening is going to have different content depending on whether you're giving it to an experienced group or someone who is just getting started in the field. Is your audience a group of business professionals or more casual? You should really take the time understand your audience. To help them connect and understand what you are saying, make sure to include all necessary information in your speech. Consider what you want the audience to do after you have spoken.

What is the Setting

This is closely linked to the audience. Will your speech be given in a business setting or in a more casual environment at a reception? Are there large audiences or small intimate groups? These are important factors to consider when preparing your speech. If you are speaking to small groups, it is important that you are more approachable.

Now that you have a clear understanding of your purpose for the speech and who your audience are, you can begin to prepare the presentation. Do not skip these vital steps in your preparation. It is important that your speech is in line with the needs of your audience. The most important thing is to keep your speech focused on the end goal.

Chapter 17: Nobody Is Perfect - Mistakes Are Guaranteed

If you've been striving for perfection in all things, then I'm afraid I'll have to break the news. You are trying capture smoke in an anet. You are more likely to find a unicorn riding T.Rex than you are of creating or creating something truly special.

We can't really attain perfection on any level other than what is useful for us daily. We humans cannot achieve dazzling perfection on any other level than the coarse measurement.

If you find yourself struggling to complete tasks and projects on time, sometimes even failing to do so, you might be a perfectionist. Perfectionists will be those who are constantly striving to achieve perfection before moving forward. If you are good at setting goals, taking action and finishing the job on time, but bad at finishing it off, you will be a perfectionist.

Perfectionist traits can make you feel like you're not alone.

Who am you to criticize? I have been a perfectionist many times. I have been bogged down in all manner of ways, especially when it comes writing. I'm now on constant guard against the demons perfection.

You won't be able to finish a speech/present if it is not rehearsed. Is this going be good for your speaking nerves or not? You won't.

As a professional coach, many people have failed to complete their tasks. Many people will say that they want to please others. This is why perfectionists are so hard to find. It is easy to worry about what others might think of a less than perfect result, output, or idea. A common question is "Isn't it right and proper that we strive to produce the best output for our intended recipients of our efforts?" The answer is yes. However, the question asks about "best output you could" and not "perfect output." While this is admirable, it is ultimately misguided. This is not acceptable because the end result will never be perfect. The perfectionist will never provide anything. Everyone loses.

To claim that perfectionionism is to the benefit of other people is an exaggeration. It is a justification. It is a convenient means of placing blame on the unattainable goal. However, there may be a deeper root cause. It's a way for perfectionists cover up deeper fears.

Extreme perfectionionism, which is a combination of type one-type two fear, is an example. Perfectionists have worries and fears about their ability, which is paired with concerns about others' thoughts and judgements. This is actually a dangerous combination of fear and anxiety.

Now, what do you think? Are you an perfectionist who is afraid of failure? Do you fear failure? Do you fear success? Do you expect perfection from other people? Do you think they expect perfection of you?

Here's a reality test for you. What you have to offer and what you say is valuable and valuable, people will value it not for how it was edited or polished. It is what it really is to them. Don't be afraid to put your passion into your creations. Make them as beautiful as possible, but don't forget to polish them. Let them go out and people will listen, value, and even love them.

The Law of Diminishing Returns states that after a certain point there is less improvement relative the amount of effort put in to it. This means that if you have something that is as good as it can be, you and others will not notice a difference.

Remember, others are not perfect.

Most of the times, what you perceive as potential defects or deficiencies will not be noticed. You can't control the opinions or actions of other people so it's not worth worrying about. Ask for feedback and fix things later, if necessary.

It will take time, but you can begin now. If you can let go of all perfectionist qualities about speaking and presenting, you'll naturally have less worry and have fewer speaking nerves. As a result, your speaking skills will improve and you will speak more often. Another benefit.

Relaxation or perfection? I know which I choose now.

Now, we can reveal another potentially shocking truth.

You will make mistakes.

Sorry to be the bearer for more unpleasant news. But, this is also a solid fact and there is no escaping it.

We all make mistakes. Try anything new and you'll almost certainly make mistakes. You can avoid mistakes by doing nothing in your daily life and trying nothing new. Ever. This is not a good option, isn't it?

It's the same for speaking. You will make mistakes. You'll forget to write words, lines or whole sections. You might move too often or too slowly. You might target your material too high for your audience or too low. You may make mistakes you don't know how to make, but it is possible.

It is normal to make mistakes.

Most mistakes you make will not cause any harm. Sometimes, however, you'll make huge mistakes. The most embarrassing doozies are those that no one seems to notice. There is nowhere to hide. You can't hide. It's not uncommon for us all to have been there. It can't just be me.

Here's the thing: it is perfectly normal to reflect upon any kind of error and engage in an internal dialogue to rectify it. A post event personal de-brief if you like.

This analysis can be optimistic, pessimistic, and both. Optimism works better.

Instead of looking at the negative side of events, and dwelling on all that happened, you should first focus on the positives and then see areas for improvement. It's all about using a different inner language.

Remember in the previous chapter how to control your inner voice? This is where it gets real.

Here's the key takeaway. Be kind to yourself and don't let mistakes define you. Be kind to yourself and let yourself have some fun. Learn to be kind to yourself. It is OK to make mistakes. The real problem is when you don't learn from your errors and continue making them repeatedly.

Last but not least, remember that this type if turnaround thinking requires effort and dedication. Once you get it in the muscle, you will begin to see clear and positive results.

Successful planning is key to success

What would surprise you? Most people don't have a plan. Some people plan nothing at all. I will be the first person to admit that most plans end up failing as soon as they get in touch with the real-world. However, these plans provide a good guideline for any activity. Do you plan to do more after you have been granted permission for a gig, or a presentation? Do you try to plan as much as possible or just do nothing and hope everything turns out okay? Which is your favorite?

Let's talk about success planning.

Here is a critical consideration to include in your success planning.

Planning for success doesn't just mean looking at the desired outcomes, but also how to get there. Effective planning involves making a realistic assessment of possible problems, and then pre-planning to solve them or avoid them. These will help to ensure they are not a major surprise. This is taking an action-oriented, future-positive attitude to deal with any negative events to reach your positive goals.

There are three levels of planning that I would recommend as minimum. Each type of planning is tied to the timeframe and each one will assist you as your presentation gets closer.

Level one refers to the long-range planning. This is essentially the description of the whole presentation activity and all the steps necessary to achieve it.

A level one presentation plan could contain all the information you need to deliver your message. These details could include dates, times, venues, etc... but they should also cover the scope of the presentation both from the viewpoint of the organisers or you as the speaker. What do they want? How can your abilities to assist them?

This plan should detail the steps you will need before you take the stage. This could be the preparation of the presentation, travel arrangements and material arrangement. Each of these tasks will come with several sub-categories. Preparing a presentation would, for example, include everything needed to create and deliver the presentation.

Make sure to pay attention to any potential roadblocks, or danger points.

It might be worth asking myself what I could do in the unthinkable, but not impossible, event that I fall ill before the event. I do not wish to disappoint my client so I could look into possible replacements and possibly check their availability.

Each presentation is different. Every presentation has a different priority. This means you have to constantly make judgment calls.

Level two refers to your medium range planning. This is where specific milestones can be placed, along with task completions or stages. Finally, this level allows you to check the progress of your plan against actual results.

Let's say I received notice that a presentation was scheduled for four months in the future. If this happens, I will immediately start to plan my long-term strategy. After that, I might create a three-month-to-go stage with goals relating to my progress towards delivering the speech. If I had to write my speech, research suitable travel options, and create a outline for a handout, it might be that I would need to do this. I might then create a two to three-month stage plan, a one to one stage plan, and maybe even a two to four week stage plan, depending on how important the speech is. Make sure you are aware of all possible roadblocks, and any solutions.

You can select your own milestones, according to the timescale and your personal speech design.

Finally, we get to your short term plan or plans. I say plans because I am an inveterate organizer. I have many checklists. I make "to do" lists for everything. As I get older, I find it easier to remember things so that I do not forget them, I outsource my brain and use lots of clipboards and planning whiteboards. It's all very manual and old-fashioned I admit, but that is because I am an old school type of guy. The good news is that these checklists can be reused again and again after they are completed. I am old-fashioned but I don't like working any harder than necessary. If you enjoy spreadsheets, and other electronic techy items, then go ahead. You might think project planning software is too complex. However, if you like it and it works for your purposes then you can use it.

I have an old-fashioned folder system of paper for my speaking planning. Each speaking gig gets a folder, complete with planning sheets. I seldom forget anything these days. This increases my confidence which in turn benefits both my audiences, as well the many economic buyers who hire my services. When they're happy, the economic buyers will rehire my services.

I encourage you to list everything and check all boxes before you set out. You don't want to leave anything to chance.

I've been there. And I've learned a lot. I have many different adaptors for laptops to audio visual (AV), spare batteries and memory sticks. You never know what might happen. I carry one tablet and one computer with me to every job. I also bring three USB sticks to backup my presentation. Technology fails. Don't forget to get the numbers of all venue and organiser contacts. They can be very helpful in case something unexpected happens. Remember to charge your smartphone and keep it charged until you begin the job.

Unexpected events are possible and almost always happen.

I don't wish to sound like a repetitive prophet of doom but failure to plan is the best way to fail. Anxiety and fear from not being prepared for all eventualities can be a sign of nerves that you don't want.

If you take care of your body and are open to the idea of planning for success, you will find that speaking and presenting nerves go away like morning mist.

Action points in chapters

Make a plan to make your next speaking event a success. You will be able to use this strategy every time. Make a flowchart, or write it down. You can laminate it and stick to a place where you can easily see it. It makes it much easier for you to do the right and good things.

A variety of checklists can be created for different stages. Imagine creating a folder per speaking gig. Be sure to record your work flow, plan stages and follow it. Use your checklists and complete them.

What other preparations do you think would be necessary to be more prepared, and thus less nervous?

Add it to your plan, and give it another go. You can adapt and modify each project as it is completed.

If it is working for you, keep using it. If it does not perform as planned, do not hesitate to change it. Keep trying until you get it to work.

Consider asking trusted speakers friends for advice if you need it. Everyone is not an island.

What other planning skills are you able to apply to your speaking preparations

Forewarned, forearmed.

Chapter 18: How to Give a Dynamic Speech

Your introduction sets the tone to follow. You can see how important it is that you get it right in the first few minutes. Before you can utter even one word, pay close attention to your appearance. Public perception is one the five pillars for effective public speaking. It is essential that your outfit conveys a clear message and does not distract your audience. Instead, you should make sure that your outfit is focused on your audience. This is the first element of creating a dynamic entrance. We'll start with this.

1. The Part

If you don't have a very strong point, wearing garish attire on stage can distract the audience from your message. The role of dressing the part doesn't require you to choose the first outfit on the runway. It means being consistent with your message. Simpler is better for professional events. For professional events, a well-ironed shirt should be paired with well-tailored pants and formal footwear. Put on a nice blazer for a more formal look. Try this semi-casual look: Do as professionals do. For a semi casual look, swap out your formal pants and wear khakis. Choose neutral or nude shoes for a comfortable look. Keep the rest of your outfit to the professional group. There should be no excessive jewelry, or outlandish colours. Also, avoid patterns and graphics.

2. Start with the Niceties

You must introduce yourself to anyone you meet when you first meet someone. Talk to them briefly about your identity (if they were not already familiar). It is impossible to ask the entire audience to introduce themselves. So, you should acknowledge them by giving them compliments. Try to make a positive statement about how nice they appear today. Or maybe joke about how their stern faces could be intimidating. It may not be enough to get everyone laughing, but it can make them smile. This is a great way to lift the mood in any room.

3. Go Futuristic

A lot of movie lovers will know that directors often use this technique in movies. In the beginning, the movie portrays a futuristic event, before returning to the present. The rest will walk you through the various incidents that happen and take you to the futuristic event that got you all excited. This method creates interest the instant you start to watch. You can use the same technique and ask your audience questions to create a vision of their desired future. The audience should be able see the image you are asking by answering the questions. With that image at the forefront, you are now able to guide them through the remainder of your talk.

This is just one method to ensure your audience's attention from the first time you appear on stage. There are many options for introductions. You will just need to find one that works for your needs.

Task:

Today's assignment is to go online, search for your favourite public speakers and find them on YouTube. You will find many of them at TED talk events. Pay attention for the first 5 minutes. What were the key things you noticed? Make a list of them, and then consider how you could incorporate these techniques into your presentation.

Chapter 19: The First Step Is Starting

Now, you can now picture yourself on the stage. What will be your opener? Let's rewind to "Know Your Audience". Do you want to begin with a joke (or a quote), a short story (or statistic), or something more serious? Your presentation should have an overall theme that runs throughout the time period. Consider your opener as threading that needle. Consider personalizing your opener.

Some people are naturally funny. They can deliver material with humor consistently. You can learn to be funny. Yes. Iowa State University offers the course "Comedy College." Comedy, like all other skills, is possible to learn. Second City, Chicago, offers a Training Center for all ages that helps them improve their skills in sketch comedy, improvisation, and comedy.

If you don't make jokes that are relevant to your audience, it won't work. The heart races, breathing becomes shallow and the confidence starts to drop. It's not possible to die. However, you won't want to miss the next 9 or 15 minutes and 15 seconds. Recall a previous tip. Make sure to run your joke by someone you trust. Und a lot of fun.

A great quote can make or break your day. Many famous people have said great, important and pertinent things throughout history. Abraham Lincoln spoke one memorable speech. Did you realize that the Gettysburg Address only lasted three minutes? Did you know that Abraham Lincoln was afraid of public speaking. You are not the only one.

A short, relevant story is always a great way to get into the hearts of your readers. These two words are relevant and brief. Spending too much time on the opener could cause you to lose focus on the content of your presentation. Even if you are running a workshop lasting six hours, your opener should still be relevant.

Did you also know that glossophobia affects 74% of the population? What a wonderful statistic. Do you think your audience knows what glossophobia means? You will, because I mention it in the book. 74% of people are afraid of speaking in public. Statistics are an excellent way to attract your audience. Keep in mind that you should only start your presentation by presenting a couple of statistics. Unless it's important. You're talking to college students interested in the sciences. Then get into statistics. They love it!

A Friday seminar I gave for leaders in Parramatta on how to manage problem employees was something that I enjoyed. Parramatta can be described as a business area in the greater metropolitan area of

Sydney. Sydney and Melbourne were set to take part in Rugby finals on that weekend.

Australians are sports lovers. The Aussies enjoy cheering at sporting events. One half of the crowd yells "Aussie", Aussie. Aussie!" The other half yells: "Oy Oy Oy!" I guarantee you this is the sound you will hear when you next watch any Australian sporting event.

I began the day by reminding them that I was aware of their match with Melbourne. I let them know that I was aware of their match with Melbourne and wanted to ensure I was cheering appropriately during the match. I repeated "Aussie", Aussie, Aussie" and they responded loudly, "Oy Oy Oy!" The Banquet manager inspected everything and poked his head through all the doors. I gave him the thumbs up, and he grinned from head to ear. Even he knew this was going to a great day. The day was at the same level throughout. This is still one the best openings to an extraordinary day.

Keep in mind how long the presentation will last when you choose your opener. If you are making a toast, the opener would simply be to explain how you are connected. Perhaps you could break down your 10-minute presentation into 3 categories. The opener should be no more than one or two minutes. The body of your presentation will be about six minutes long. You will then have two minutes left to wrap it up. This is just an example. You can separate it in any way that you like.

On the other hand, if you are hosting a workshop lasting several hour, or a full day of presentations, you will want to devote about ten seconds to your opener. This opener will give you credibility to show the audience why your subject is important and how you plan on keeping their attention.

No matter how you start, create a welcome that sets the tone of the presentation. I referred back to Stephen Covey's practice of "Begin Without the End In Thought" during my introduction. If you have trouble deciding how to present your presentation, it is worth starting by creating the concept. Take the time to go through all of the content and endings and then come back to your opener.

Chapter 20: Evaluation

Honesty is best policy

Actors need to be able to assess themselves and make improvements. It is difficult to improve if we aren't able to watch ourselves perform and give ourselves criticism. It's the exact same with public speaking.

You can self-evaluate by recording yourself speaking. Recordings can be taken in practice, or in a real scenario. Many speeches are recorded automatically by companies. Ask for a copy.), and then evaluate the impact of your speech based upon the elements described in the first six chapters.

You've done all the preparation, but this is what really matters. This section is not a place to do exercises. However, it does provide a guideline to self-evaluation.

Where do I start?

The self-evaluation table on the next page was created so you can analyze and criticize every aspect of how your presentation skills are doing. This will enable you to identify and critique the areas you are still working on.

In each of the 16 areas you can mark yourself and tell others, "My speech sounds good but my posture and gestures could be improved." This is so much more than simply saying, "Well that could of been better," after a presentation. Or listening to people saying, "You're great!"

Although it can be beneficial to receive praise from colleagues, their biases are likely. Being honest with oneself and watching your back is the best way to do this.

Self-Evaluation

It is a good idea to copy the table below so you can quickly record your scores.

What the Scores mean

Add all of the scores you get after marking yourself on everything, you will get a number from 16 to 160.

16-64 : It is probable that you lack self-confidence, which could be negatively affecting your performance. Working on your weaknesses separately can increase your impact and help you to present a confident, high-status persona.

65-126 It's possible to improve in one of the areas you have scored 1 or 2 and help in others.

127-160 : Congratulations. Your presentation was outstanding. There are likely only a few points that can be improved. Don't forget that there's always improvement to be made, so don't get complacent.

Breathing Breathing

Unregulated /10 controlled

Shallow/10 Deep

Posture Posture

Uncomfortable/10 Comfortable

Slouched / Straight Backed

Stiff/10 Relaxed

Status

Fidgety/10 Calm

Random Gestures /10 Purposeful Gestures

Gestures Irrelevant to words /10 Gestures Enhanced speech

Vocals Vocals

Fast Speech/10 Well-Paced Talk

Many Verbal Crutches ('uh') /10 Few Verbal Crutches

No Pauses/10 Well Placed Pauses

No Inflection/Overinflection/10 Well Judged Iflection

Shouting /10 Appropriate projection

Articulation Articulation

Slurred Speech/10 Clear Voice

Other

No Eye Contact /10 Good/Clear Eye Contact

Notes became an obstacle.

A Few Final Tips...

After going through this guide's sections and exercises, you might think: "I have a lot of things to remember." But don't worry. Practice makes perfect. You'll get better at speaking the more you practice. This guide offers tips to help you improve quickly from experts who have used the exercises to their advantage.

However, there are still important things to communicate before you stand up on stage.

These things are less about how technical your performance is and more about what can be done to improve the overall quality your speech.

Contacts for the eyes

Eye contact can be one of the most powerful tools to get your message across.

It is essential for public speakers to have good eye contact.

First of all, do not stare at people in the audience. It won't work. Instead, deliver your message by speaking one line to each person, then finding the next one and saying the next.

Either way, you should not rush from one person or another trying to fit them all in. It will make your nervousness worse. Relax and flow naturally from one speaker to the other, letting the speech rhythm guide you.

If you are giving your speech to only one person, such as to answer questions or to address judges in a courtroom setting, be attentive to their needs and respond. Don't look around trying to find the answer. You must stay focused.

Handling Notes

Don't make your notes your slave, instead become their master. A person's dependence on their notes can be instantly seen by an audience, which has a direct impact on how they perceive you and what your message is. Be sure to study the notes carefully so you don't need them. Refer to them only when you have to.

There are many methods for learning the entire speech, but you may not have the time or ability to use them all. If this is the case, learn to look upwards more than downwards. Even if you only need the notes for a portion of your speech, it is important to acknowledge your audience and not just read the text from the page. Eye contact is important. Keep looking up, make eye contact and pause when necessary.

It's important to actually hold your notes with confidence.

Picture It

You can counter nerves by visualising the situation ahead of time. You can sit down, close the eyes, and visualise the entire scene from getting up to going. It helps to have a clear mental image of the audience and the room so that you can give a great speech when it comes.

If you can think it out in your head, it'll be much easier when it comes to speaking in real life. As performers on stage, we do this subconsciously and constantly. This really helps to ease your nerves. However, you should be careful not to anticipate the audience's reactions. If they are unexpectedly different to your plans, you could be caught off guard. You can, however, try to imagine your response to questions and interruptions.

Don't Apologise

It is common for nervous speakers to avoid apologizing. "Sorry. It's not my normal behavior," "Sorry.

It's far better to just go with the flow. Don't be sorry for your nerves. You'll only draw attention to them. Most people won't notice you if you didn't tell them.

You are not responsible if you don't know how respond to a comment. Don't apologize, just say "I don't know how to respond" or other appropriate words.

Apologising to yourself for speaking poorly can be a sign that you aren't comfortable with your speech and yourself.

Use Your Words

You can think of what you're doing at the simplest level. For example, standing in front several other humans and speaking some words. It suddenly doesn't sound as scary! Although the words you use may sound different from your usual speech, it is still communicating a message.

It is important to forget all other things, such as the impact that a speech has on your career and public image. These are all things that will make it difficult to get ahead. Don't worry about it.

"Just saying words," can also have a literal meaning. "Erm," "Uh," and "Um" are not words. So don't say them. They won't make your speech better, and they definitely won't help your message get across.

Their Perspective

You must remember that your audience wants you to excel. If they're professionals themselves, they will be able to understand and listen to you. It's important to see it from their viewpoint. Consider how you will perceive people if you're the one listening.

Nobody is going or will be as harsh on you as yourself. Nobody is going and going to ever forget a bad experience. Don't get mad at yourself if you do make a mistake. It's okay to learn from it and move forward. Most people won't really care.

The scenario should be viewed from your perspective. However, imagine someone watching you speak from the audience's eyes. It will make it less frightening!

Take the time to enjoy the experience

Trial and error can have the biggest impact on your speaking ability. This guide can help you improve your speaking skills, but practice and learning are the only way to really grow.

Self-evaluation is an excellent tool to help you do this. This will allow you to measure your performance in each area, and show how you are progressing over time. Although practice can make perfect, it is much easier to improve when you are honest with yourself and recognize the weak points.

Although it sounds repetitive, it's important that you are assertive and willing to learn from your failures. There are many lessons you can take away from your current capabilities to make you the best version possible, but the most important is self awareness.

Chapter 21: Professional Speakers' Real Message

Is your communication really what you think it is? There are two messages that should be included in every speaking engagement: the visual message and the verbal message. Effective communication is key for professional speakers. No matter whether you are new to speaking or have years of experience, it is important that you understand your message and then adjust your delivery to achieve the best results. This will help you deliver winning presentations everytime!

The verbal communication is the first message type. Your verbal message should first be clear and concise. Your points of discussion must be specific and supported by data, testimonials, or visual aids. The flow of discussion and transition points should lead your audience to where they need to be.

Your tone of voice should support the verbal message. Tone of voice is a way to make your topic interesting. You should emphasize the key points with enthusiasm and enthusiasm. A somber voice can make it easier to identify the problems and then present a solution. A loud, booming voice can emphasize definitive statements.

The visual message forms the second type. These messages are, along with your message using your tone-of-voice, often inferred messages. But they still speak volumes about who you are as a leader.

Your presentation's environment has a direct impact on how you deliver your message. You could lose your attention and lose your focus in a noisy environment. Even though it might seem that things like the room temperature (too hot, too cold) or traffic noises (beeping and sirens), are beyond your control, there are some things you can do. Another important environmental factor is the room's appearance. Is the room professional? Is the interior warm and inviting? Does it reinforce the message that you want to send or do they take away? It is your responsibility to keep distractions out of your presentation as minimal as possible.

Another visual presentation you can make is one that features your personal appearance. Your audience doesn't know anything about you. Do you present yourself as a professional? You don't have have to own the Armani suits, or the Dolce & Gabbana clothes. But you do have to present yourself as a professional. The loudest colors should be avoided by men speakers. If you are going out for the evening, don't wear loud colored shirts. The best way to dress for women is to be conservative. It doesn't matter if you're wearing a burlap-sack, but it is important to dress conservatively. Your goal is credibility as a professional.

Your audience will also pick up other messages throughout your presentation. They can tell by your enthusiasm how you feel about the topic. They already make assumptions about your credibility, as a true professional. Don't make mistakes and send the wrong message.

Props to Enhance Your Professional Speaking Presentation

Information is learned and retained differently by different people. In order to reach as many people possible as professional speakers, you need to learn to integrate as many ways to engage your audience. Your obligation is to use everything you can to connect your message with people's lives. Props are a part of every message you send.

If you touch or use an object while on stage, it is called a "prop". Props may include flip charts or demonstrations, overhead projections (images, photos, videos) and even other people. Props are a great way to enhance the message you're trying to send to your audience.

Props encourage your audience to become more involved in your presentation. Props help you to connect with your audience.

They can be visual illustrations which are more powerful than words and are often able to communicate the message. It is one thing for people to hear your new idea. But, when they see it visually, they can form a mental image of the idea in their minds and become more connected to what you are trying. Visual presentations can help you make your points more interesting, and break up the monotony of just listening to what you say. Props can be added to variety your presentation.

Giving away prizes and other giveaways makes a great opening prop. Props are a great way for large audiences to be opened, especially in large venues. The props are a great way to get your audience excited about the subject matter you are going on. The prizes could be related or unrelated to your message. You can use them to break up the conversation or to get attention to your support materials sales in the back.

Props can be used as an "impromptu" part of your presentation. Props, when used properly, can keep your audience on their toes as they watch you work in front of them. You won't be reading a speech while talking about your props. They can also serve as notes substitutes because they prompt the user to explain why they are introducing the prop. Props can help you go through an entire presentation.

Props can be a great addition to your presentation. Visual images are better than words. You can also show your audience what points you are trying make, rather than simply repeating them. You've heard the expression, "A picture speaks louder than a thousand words." Props can also be used to excite and inspire your audience, as well as warm them up for your presentation. Try using props to engage your audience in your presentation.

Where to Look When You Speak

When giving a speech or giving a presentation, the body language you use and how you conduct yourself in front people speaks volumes as much as what you say. When you're speaking publicly, it is important not to act nervous. If you have complete control on your body as well as your hands, then you can relax and be relaxed in front of others. As a result, you will be able to deliver your speech more easily.

Public speakers are often plagued by poor eye use. Public speakers are prone to looking at the outline of their speech and writing throughout their presentations. It can be very easy to lose track or feel like you don't know what they are saying next. This is why many people who don't have the ability to talk in front a crowd write their speeches word for word, and then just read it out to the group.

Problem with this approach is that you were asked to give an address, not a reading. Many adults find it offensive to be read to. Your audience wants to hear something from you, not just your reading. If that was your only purpose for a public talk, you could just give out your speech as a whitepaper to the audience and let them go through it. However, public speaking is much more effective than handing out a white paper. This is especially true if your speech's purpose is to convince people or sell.

This raises the question of where to look while you give your speech. Many speakers find it difficult to see the faces of others in the room so they look at them. This is better then staring at your paper the entire time. Projection is a key part in getting your message out. Even if you use a microphone to communicate, if it is "out" you speak into the crowd, rather than down, your voice and diaphragm will sound clearer.

If you're not using amplification, the other benefit of looking at a back wall is that it can help you project yourself. Here, "Performing to the Last Row" refers to acting. This means you should consider all the people in the hall to be your audience. It is a good idea.

Make eye contact with your audience to build rapport and communicate your message. A salesperson will often make eye contact with customers to create a connection and help close the deal. Even if your presentation doesn't involve sales, eye contacts will convey your message. This is what you went up to in the first instance.

Eye contact can make your audience look at and pay attention to you. It keeps them awake and alert. To maximize the value of eye contact, look from one audience member towards another remembering to then talk to the person directly. Eye contact with an individual is felt by all around them and will captivate the listener. While you may not want to stare at anyone, it is important to be able to use eye contact to communicate with others. This will allow you to control the presentation and direct it in the direction you wish. This is the key to success in public speaking.

What's Your Problem

You have to think about why you are giving the speech. How you approach it will impact how you present. It's not that your boss requires you to give a speech to pass your junior college speech class. In order to deliver a strong speech, you have to be able to clearly understand what the speech is intended to do. The goal of the speech and what you want the audience experience from your presentation will give you valuable information. It will also help you determine your "approach" and attitude when you are actually preparing to deliver the talk.

It is not necessary that someone give a speech. They are to inform. To convince. To amuse. Or to cause action. These motivations can be found in many speeches. A sermon is intended as an inspiration. It is a combination to convince and cause people to take action. A lecture in school is intended to inform. If you are fortunate, the teacher will also attempt to entertain. Once you have identified your topic and your audience, that is the most important question. There are also variations to these themes. A speech meant to sell something is another variation on the "to convince" format.

The best question you can ask before you begin to put together your presentation is "What should my audience do with this information?" You spoke to inform if your goal is for them to leave with more knowledge and a better understanding of the subject. If you want them laughing and having a good time, then you were trying to entertain. Your goal is to convince them to go to your web site, to sign up for your political party, and to stop damaging the ozone layers.

It's not essential that you announce when speaking your objective. Sometimes it is clear. It's obvious that you are trying to inform students when you address them in class. The information you give may not only inform, but also convince them to take a different action. A speech for amusement is often also a sermon on behavior. Any comedian will share a few bits of philosophy during their comedy set. The comic is actually trying to change you and your outlook using comedy.

These are all valid variations on the basic speech forms. Your talk should reach its primary topic. To ensure your talk is successful, you must outline the outline (or "skeleton") of the speech keeping your primary goal at heart. Perhaps you could even "back into your talk" by writing the concluding sentence first. Let's say, "And now, ladies, and gentlemen. Mass transit will greatly help the ozone Layer." Once you have this information, you can move on to the body and tell the skeleton layer about your three main points. These are what you should do. Then you will be able to evaluate your success by how well you did.

Once you have that outline, you can write the speech. To make your speech memorable, captivating and engaging, you can add humor, urban myths, factsoids or historical information.

If you feel that you reached your primary goal by the time you finish your talk, then your speech is well constructed. A well-constructed speech will be easier to deliver. It is also easier to communicate with your audience so that everyone wins.

Put Some Snap Into It.

A public speaking presentation can be boring and entertaining. But the difference between one that bores you and one that makes you smile and think about the topic is often the style of its speaker. You can take the same script and give it to 2 speakers. The first will make it an exciting live event and the second will make it boring.

The goal of any speaker is to bring life to a presentation. It is important to realize that the ability to generate excitement is not a function of the subject matter. While it is good to be excited about your topic, you can also learn skills that will allow you to turn any text into an engaging public speaking event. It is all about learning how.

A lot of the excitement you get from your audience comes down to how high your energy is, your senses of humor, and how much time you have having fun. This is one thing that makes great entertainers and public speakers. Your audience will enjoy having fun if you have fun. Fun is contagious. Johnnie Carson was the great late-night host. He seemed to always have a great time. It was obvious that the rest of the world wanted to enjoy his great times and be there too. You can bring that attitude and personality to the stage.

Public speaking should be fun. This can be challenging if the subject matter seems boring or repetitive. Talking to boring people will make your life miserable. It doesn't matter how mundane the topic might be, have some fun. By joining the audience's feelings about the topic, both you and them can experience the joy of this topic.

It is important to find joy in the topic. You also need to be able have fun and enjoy the company of the audience. Before you even begin to discuss the outline, you can have fun with the audience. Spend some time interacting with the audience, away from your podium. Ask them questions, and you will learn which of the crowd members are the most vocal. Find out which jokers you can trust and which ones have some wisdom to share.

These connections and spontaneous friendships will pay dividends once the presentation starts. But be aware that you're also taking a risk. Energizing the crowd is a way to give them permission for their talk to be a success. Use energy, humor, passion, and personality as you speak. The crowd will love you for sharing your love with them and your humor with them will fuel your presentation.

Yes, this kind of snap-and-pop approach to your talk will bring back feedback from the audience, especially from those wise crackers whom you took the time to get to know. As frightening as this type of interruption may be, it can also mean that your crowd is energized. You can even use it to your advantage. You can actually learn to'surf these interruptions and make use of them to propel your prevention forward. Asking questions to the crowd and teasing them, you can get funny comments back that will relate to your next message. Take your cues and draw from their comments. Then, you can bring them back to your outline to complete the presentation.

This type of public speaking can be dangerous, and it can be difficult to master. But, because you had fun and everyone had fun, the presentation was a lot more successful and full of snap. That's why it is worth taking risks learning public speaking.

Chapter 22: Humor

Why not use humor in public speaking? It's a great way to add humor to your presentation. It has great value.

There are many uses for it. As we all know there are many uses for it.

There's a certain amount of nervousness in both the presenter, and the audience.

The audience. Use of appropriate humor can relax the audience

It is more inviting and comfortable for the audience

As the presenter. Humor can bring out the best in you.

Pay attention and pay close attention to the message you are trying convey.

You can help your audience remember your message better.

Humor can bring down barriers, so that the audience is more open to it.

They are more open to your suggestions. When you use

Humor in public settings is especially useful when you are dealing with others.

You're speaking to a business audience.

Audience that isn't specifically there

Humor, use humor to strengthen your point

This will ensure that you get a better response.

It is a good idea for your presentation to begin with humor. This is called a "ho-humcrasher". This will relax you as well as the audience. Use humor to open your presentation. Listen to their reactions and see if you need to adjust.

The best and most efficient way to find humor in a presentation is through your own experiences. Safe humor is vital. Remember that humor used outside of the "you" persona can backfire. Please exercise caution. You are the most trustworthy person to use as the point for the humor. Reflect on a time you felt embarrassed and thought it wasn't funny. However, if you look back at the incident now, it's funny and you can now laugh about it. This humor is great to share and enjoy with your audience. It's called the "Stoop Factor" and it simply refers to something I did, that was actually stupid. This is typically safe humor because it's not about you.

You have to find humor that is enjoyable for you. If you don't find humor funny, your audience won't either. You should only use humor that makes your heart smile or makes you laugh. I use humor in my presentations, because I love what you do. I also have fun when presenting. It's even possible to get paid for it.

Make sure to test humor in a small group before you present it. Did they find it funny and enjoyable? Don't be discouraged if the group doesn't smile or laugh at first. It could just be the way the humor was delivered. You'll get there if you keep practicing. Nothing is worse than listening in to a boring, boring speaker. Don't be shy! Bring some humor and fire to the table!

Make sure your humor is pertinent to your message. Use humor that is not intended to make the audience smile. Comedy is not just for comedians. You must tie the humor to some portion of the presentation so that the audience can enjoy the humor while also remembering the point.

Use humor that is shared by people you are close to. You do not need to be concerned about others hearing it. It is easier to accept what has happened. Try to find a funny line or situation.

We have spoken a lot on the value of humor. But how does it get delivered? There are many ways you can achieve this. The key thing is to understand when and how to deliver it. Let's start with the "punch" line.

A punchline refers to the final part or a sentence of a joke. It's usually the word, sentence and exchange of sentences. It is intended to cause laughter among listeners. This is not a difficult technique to learn. Your punch line is delivered in a slightly more difficult and different manner than the rest. You may find it helpful to lean in front of the microphone and repeat the punchline louder and clearly than you did the set lines. If they do not hear the punch lines, they are unlikely to laugh. The punch line should be emphasized and drawn to special attention by pauses just before it.

You should not make a sound until you have completed the line. Give the audience a chance for a laugh. This is difficult as you might feel compelled to add to the punchline if there isn't an immediate response. Keep calm and wait. Waiting for more experience is the hardest part until you get better. A lot of public speakers are afraid that no laughter will be forthcoming, so they keep on speaking. If you talk too much, it will be easy to kill the laughter. As you succeed in this area, your confidence increases and pausing becomes more common. Sometimes the audience will laugh, even if you don't have the best joke. The punch line is now covered and we are ready to deliver it. But who do you deliver it to, anyway?

Only one person should hear your punch line. It doesn't matter how big the audience is. You can just look one person in their eyes and deliver your punchline. Pick someone carefully. Doing so can lead to problems. Chapter 10 is about meeting attendees and meeting them before the presentation. It is important that you meet with participants to find out what they think and be open to your humor. Find out where the participants are sitting. That way, you will be able to see them clearly during your presentation. Your general rule is to deliver your punchlines only to people you know are going to laugh. Watch the audience at every opportunity before you present. There will be many opportunities throughout the program before you are able to present.

A coordinator, or M/C, is a speaker. It is important to understand the dance floor before getting up and dancing.

Let's start with a simple idea: the head nod. Those who really understand what you are talking about will nod their heads gently in approval. These people should be sought out as you can have great success with humor delivery.

You can influence your audience with humorous lines that will make them laugh. There are two reasons you might do this. Importantly, you want the audience to see the "laugher", and follow their lead. If you aim humor at a person in the audience who is laughing, it will be a natural result that others will do the same and have a higher chance of having a good time. Your confidence is another reason to give your punch line if you are confident. Don't let fear get in the way of your ability to deliver your punch line to someone who isn't familiar with it. You must deliver your humor to people who will enjoy it.

Humor is an additional way to reach your audience and can make you a better speaker. Consider humor as a tool for improving your presentation.

Now that we have the what, how about how? You can make or ruin a joke by how you deliver it. Don't reveal your punchline. If the humor of your punch line is dependent upon the words you used in the introduction, don't use them. "Never repeat a punchline, explain your joke or repeat it. You have failed, botched it or failed to deliver, so forget it! It is important to memorize the punch line. This is your personal name. The better punch line is shorter. An interminable punch line can turn off the audience. Let's talk about punch. Simply, punch means forcefulness, effectiveness, or pungency with regard to content or appeal. Nothing is said about a slow, slow, or lumbering act. Your punch line needs to be quick, strong and short. Just practice! Practice! Practice!

All public speakers are familiar with the rule-of-three and I want everyone to know it. Three jokes and one-liners on a single topic are sufficient to increase the audience's interest, but not enough that they become bored about the subject. Experts suggest that you shouldn't make fun of your own jokes, stories, or presentations in public. This is a good rule. It is a fact that every time I speak, I make something funny and silly. I just cannot help but laugh when it happens. I really try to stop. And when I do, I look at the audience and do something that makes them laugh even harder. Understanding that I don't do this deliberately, I wouldn't recommend planning to include an "I did stupid thing" into your presentation. Your personality and your enthusiasm should be evident to your audience. You may find humor easy to come by, but don't force it.

The opposite is a dry expression. This is a serious expression that's contrasted to funny lines. This creates a larger laugh than a line of its own. I've used this technique many times with great success. Public speaking is a great opportunity to have fun and let loose. Your audience will appreciate your presentation more than you. This is the bottom line: Be yourself, don't force it.

You see that humor can be a valuable tool in public speaking. We have discussed the reasons for and methods of using humor. How to recognize your audience and how to apply humor to them with the minimum risk.

There are many benefits to using humor in your speech. Remember, these benefits can only help with your ultimate purpose of giving the presentation. The main thing about humor and when to use it is, is to just be you and have fun.

Straight Talk

It is simply what I did that was stupid.

"I use humor for my presentations because I love what it is and have fun when presenting. I even get paid for it!

There's nothing worse than listening in to a boring, nonentertaining speaker. Don't be shy! Bring some humor and fire to the table!

The rule of thumb is to deliver your punchlines to anyone you know will laugh.

Let's just shut up and wait.

The bottom line is to get to know the dance floor well before you dance. "Don't repeat a punchline again or tell a joke. You botched, bombed or failed to deliver, so let it go!

"Never lose the punch line!"

Let your personality shine through to your audience. If humor is something you find naturally, great! But don't force humor. You can't force humor, just be you!

Chapter 23: The Speech Opening: A Spark is the Best Start

"Things work best at the beginning"

- Blaise Pascal

"Early impressions" are difficult to get out of the mind. Who can make wool white again after it has been dyed a purple color?

- St. Jerome

Your speech's opening speech is vital for success. It is essential that the speaker arranges his introduction thoughtfully in today's world of decreasing attention spans and instant distractions, such as cell phone. In 30 seconds, the audience is likely to judge a speaker. If one fails create an impression and hook the crowd, it can be difficult to win them over.

Start with a spark.

The tone of your speech can be determined by the way that you begin your speech. Public speaking is not an easy task. It is easy to find world-class speeches and leaders from around the globe thanks to mass communication tools like television and 24x7 Internet. TED talks are full good speeches. This has increased the audience's expectations. Any boring start would frustrate the audience. It takes approximately three times as much effort for them to return their attention. Given their very short attention spans and numerous distractions, it is not an easy task. Get to the point quickly and impress your audience with a compelling start. The purpose of your start should be to create the platform for your speech. Becoming a celebrity speaker just for attention is a bad idea.

If you are giving a humorous speech, or do stand-up comedy at the beginning, humor or jokes is not the best way to begin. It could lead to people taking you seriously. This might portray you as a casual person who enjoys trivia. If you are confident and can be humorous, you may start with humor. Keep it short and get to the point. If something goes wrong in corporate and business setup, it is best not to do it.

How to open your Speech

(1) The Mystic Pause: A pause that signals the audience that the speaker is about to speak. An intentional, confident silence before speaking can be a powerful way for the audience to become curious and makes a subtle impact. It will enhance your presence on the platform. This shows confidence. It allows you to smile at the audience and makes eye contact. The audience is drawn into you when you pause before speaking. It allows them to feel and anticipate that something is coming.

(2) Telling a story is a great way to start a speech. A story about your topic can be a good way to start your speech. To share a personal story on courage as a topic, you could use it. Here's my personal tale about courage

The swimming pool always had one question in mind: How long would it take to procrastinate. Before the pool could answer, have courage, dear! I often walked off. I was a follower, but never took actual action. When I was in my late 20s, however, I started to question whether it was too late. I began swimming in December 2010. My senior colleague assisted me in learning, but it was not enough to make progress after 10 consecutive days. It was Saturday morning when he left for Chennai to be with his family. I was sorry that he was away. I took a risk and went by myself to the pool. I tried swimming for some time. After 30 minutes spent trying in vain, I suddenly learned to swim. Yes, I can swim alone. I was able to swim because of my determination to go alone that morning.

You can use this story to begin a topic about fear:

One day, a dog got lost and found his way into a palace's glass room. There were thousands of small mirrors covering the roof and walls. The dog saw the reflections and took them as his own. He barks at his reflections in fear and they bark back. He began to bark at his own reflection again, before he succumbed to exhaustion. Such is the state of a human being. Fear is nothing, but a false conception of reality. If we attempt to speak on the stage, our fear is also a result of our own false perceptions. We can see hundreds and thousands of eyes on us, wondering what they might think. Oh! They must be making fun or laughing at my mistakes. It is all a self-created perception.

The right stories can be used to back up your message. But, it is more effective to tell your own story. It can convince the audience the most about the topic. Because your audience will want to see how you dealt with the topic in your own life.

(3) Share interpersonal experience. Narendra Modi (Indian Prime Minister) began his speech in New York City's

Madison Square Garden, Sept. 28, by sharing his personal experience. He said,

"I was in Taiwan a few years ago. I didn't have a chief ministry back then. I also had an interpreter. After a few days of getting to know each other, he asked me "If you don't mind, may we ask you a question?" I answered "Yes, yes, I won't mind," and he repeated the question, "Are your sure you won't mind?" I responded, "No, not at all." He was still reluctant. And then he said, "I've heard that India was a country of black magic and snakes, charmers, and people play around with serpents; Is that true?" I replied, "No. Not anymore." Since then, we have seen a lot of progress in our country. Our ancestors used a snake as a plaything, but today the mouse is our friend."

This was a great way of highlighting the progress of India new. It displayed the power and potential of Indian youth to elevate the country. It was funny, with a powerful message. It is important that this personal experience be chosen so that audience members can relate to their own experiences.

(4) Asking a striking question: A bang is another way to get a speech started. It's a common mistake that novices make, and they end up being completely disappointed. It's easy to overlook the fact that it is difficult to get a response from the audience if the speaker does not create a good impression and build trust with them. To attract a positive response, the speaker has to be confident in their delivery and make a connection to the audience.

The questions should be universal and open to all, so that the majority of the audience agrees with them. Here are a few examples: How many people do you think can do more with your existing resources and time than you currently have?

How many of us believe our talent surpasses our current jobs or income?

How many of you want to live an active life?

How many people do you consider health extremely important?

(5) Startling statistics, facts: A good way of grabbing attention is to begin by quoting an amazing fact related to your topic. These facts and statistics should be unusual and striking. It is best not to explain the statement too much. Its utility is to spark curiosity, stimulate thoughts and feelings toward the topic. "The most important part of intellectual training is not learning facts, but how to make them live." (Oliver Wendell Holmes - American Judge).

Road accidents in India kill approximately 2100 people each week. This is almost four times the number killed by terrorists in a single year.

Indian godowns are responsible for wasting 500 miliion tonnes (40%) of total food grains due to pests or climatic conditions. This is enough food to feed half of the country for one year.

70% of Indians suffer from obesity. 80% India's women are anemic.

(6) Use an object or action as a prop. The prop could be a pen and tie, an envelope or note, Identity card, currency note, etc. depending on what topic you are addressing.

Conclusion

I hope this book can help you understand what to do if your fear of public speaking haunts.

Next, ensure you are following the advice in this book. Remember, your brain is bigger than your nerves. Do not allow them to control your life. No matter who your background is, you can be a public speaker.

www.ingramcontent.com/pod-product-compliance
Lightning Source LLC
Chambersburg PA
CBHW071838080526
44589CB00012B/1046